Promoting African American Writers

PROMOTING AFRICAN AMERICAN WRITERS

Library Partnerships for Outreach, Programming, and Literacy

Grace M. Jackson-Brown

LIBRARIES
UNLIMITED®
An Imprint of ABC-CLIO, LLC
Santa Barbara, California • Denver, Colorado

Library of Congress Cataloging-in-Publication Data

Names: Jackson-Brown, Grace, author.
Title: Promoting African American writers : library partnerships for
    outreach, programming, and literacy / Grace M. Jackson-Brown.
Description: Santa Barbara, California : Libraries Unlimited, [2023] |
    Includes bibliographical references and index.
Identifiers: LCCN 2022023642 (print) | LCCN 2022023643 (ebook) |
    ISBN 9781440870279 (paperback) | ISBN 9781440870286 (ebook)
Subjects: LCSH: Libraries—Activity programs—United States. | Academic
    libraries—Activity programs—United States. | School
    libraries—Activity programs—United States. | American
    literature—African American authors—Study and teaching—Activity
    programs. | African Americans—Study and teaching—Activity programs. |
    Libraries—United States—Marketing. | Library outreach programs—United
    States—Case studies. | Libraries and community—United States—Case
    studies. | Libraries—Cultural programs—United States—Case studies. |
    BISAC: LANGUAGE ARTS & DISCIPLINES / Library & Information Science /
    General | LITERARY COLLECTIONS / American / African American & Black |
    LCGFT: Case studies.
Classification: LCC Z716.33 J33 2023 (print) | LCC Z716.33 (ebook) |
    DDC 025.5—dc23/eng/20220610
LC record available at https://lccn.loc.gov/2022023642
LC ebook record available at https://lccn.loc.gov/2022023643

ISBN: 978-1-4408-7027-9 (print)
       978-1-4408-7028-6 (ebook)

27 26 25 24 23   1 2 3 4 5

This book is also available as an eBook.

Libraries Unlimited
An Imprint of ABC-CLIO, LLC

ABC-CLIO, LLC
147 Castilian Drive
Santa Barbara, California 93117
www.abc-clio.com

This book is printed on acid-free paper ∞

Manufactured in the United States of America

Contents

Acknowledgments   vii

Introduction   ix

Chapter 1. Working Together for Library Outreach:
Promoting African American Writers   1

Chapter 2. The National African American Read-In:
A Model Program That Works   17

Chapter 3. Building Partnerships and Developing
Programs That Promote African American Writers   29

Chapter 4. Identifying African American Writers for Programs   53

Chapter 5. Library Programming Assessment and
African American Writer Programs   81

Chapter 6. Reflective and Intentional Programming to
Promote African American Writers   95

Conclusion   113

*Appendix: Brief Biographies of African American
Writers and Culture Keepers*   119

Index   143

Acknowledgments

I wish to acknowledge and express my deep gratitude to my partners over the years in providing library programming that promoted African American writers. Thank you to Marianna Brough, who was the coordinator of the Neal-Marshall Black Culture Center (NMBCC) Library while I served as the head of the NMBCC Library at Indiana University. Thank you to the members of the Springfield African American Read-In Committee for the many years that we worked together in bringing programs that celebrated African American authors in Springfield: Lola Butcher, Cheryl Clay, Heather Cottle, Nora England, Charlotte Hardin, Martha Love, Gwendolyn Marshall, Eva Pelkey, and Rosalyn Thomas.

Introduction

WHY I WRITE THIS BOOK

I write this book for the purpose of sharing ideas about programming that I hope will help other librarians and educators. In the book, I reflect on my experience of more than thirty years as an academic librarian who has a passion for developing cultural and educational programs for library outreach. My experience has been focused primarily on programs on African American culture, and in that regard this book may be considered a personal career ethnography. On the other hand, it is filled with scores of practical programming tips so that the text may be viewed as a general "how-to" reference or guidebook. Throughout the book I share case examples that I collected from librarians from across the country about how they conducted special programs, including during the two-year (2020 and 2021) COVID-19 pandemic.

I didn't start my career as a programming librarian. Before my introduction to library programming, I served in other library roles.

Here's a brief description of my journey. I was born and raised in the college town of Lawrence, Kansas (Rock Chalk Jayhawks!). I have lived in the Midwest all my life, interchanging residency in the states of Kansas, Ohio, Indiana, and Missouri. In my first library employment, I worked as a student assistant at Watson Library while enrolled at the University of Kansas (KU). I married just prior to my senior year at KU. After some time, I enrolled and transferred my course credits to the University of Missouri-Kansas City (UMKC). I earned a bachelor's degree in English, with an emphasis in journalism, from UMKC. I continued my education by earning a master's degree in library and information management from Emporia State University in Emporia Kansas. There I worked as a graduate student assistant for a women's resource center that had a small collection of books and other materials.

I began my professional librarian career in Ohio. I served as head of access services, or head of circulation and reserves, as it was called back then, at King Library at Miami University of Ohio in Oxford. I worked at the university for about two years. From there, my family (husband and young daughter and I) moved to Bloomington, Indiana, where my husband went to graduate school at Indiana University (IU). While he was in graduate school, he served as a live-in coordinator for a residence hall, the John W. Ashton Center. Members of my family can tell many captivating stories of our experiences living for five years in the residence hall, or dormitory as it is called by some, which makes my husband wince. I became pregnant after our first full year of living at Ashton Center. My husband and I had our second child, a son, who was born and raised a Hoosier! After my son turned two years of age, I began working part-time as a reference librarian for the Monroe County Public Library in Bloomington. I was employed at the library for about three years. Then I applied and was hired as a reference librarian with the Main Library of IU. After earning tenure at IU-Bloomington as a librarian faculty member, I was promoted to the head of the campus library in IU's Black Culture Center, which was home to the African American Arts Institute and other offices. The African American Arts Institute is composed of a choral ensemble, dance company, and the IU Soul Revue (a popular music performing group). It was in this environment that I became an enthusiast for cultural and educational library outreach programming.

While I served as the director of the library of the Black Culture Center, the facility grew and expanded in size and services. A major change was that the library moved into a newly constructed building in 2002, into a shared space with IU's newly renovated Theatre and Drama Department. The renovated and newly constructed space for the Theatre and Drama Center combined physically with the newly built Black Culture Center in a unique architecturally designed facility. The new complex included three theatres, classrooms, offices, a dance studio, and a library. In a two-day ceremony, the complex opened with two special guests, theatre and screen legends Ossie Davis and Ruby Dee.

Soon after it opened, the Black Culture Center was renamed the Neal-Marshall Black Culture Center (NMBCC) after IU's first African American male graduate (Marcellus Neal) and African American female graduate (Frances Marshall), in 1895 and 1919, respectively. It was as head of the library in the NMBCC that I honed my programming skills. My experiences in serving in and directing the NMBCC Library and my involvement in other areas at IU led to my trajectory as a leader of educational programming for academic library outreach, which grew into my personal passion.

In 2007, my family and I moved to the "Show-Me-State" of Missouri and the city of Springfield. There I helped to build a "town and gown" literacy initiative known as the Springfield African American Read-In. Much of my motivation in the latter endeavor grew from the early inspiration that I had found by developing programming for the library in the NMBCC at IU-Bloomington. It was there that I first learned of and observed the African American Read-In (AARI) event. This was led by then IU assistant professor in the School of Education, Stephanie Power-Carter.

The AARI is not limited to any one locality. It is a national literacy program that originated with the Black Caucus of the National Council of Teachers of English in 1989. The national founder of the AARI, Dr. Jerrie Cobb Scott, wanted to make reading an integral part of Black History Month. After moving to Springfield, I soon learned that an African American Read-In had been piloted at one middle school. I became involved there in the AARI and was soon elected chairperson. I helped to build the Springfield AARI into a collaborative partnership of several organizations committed to forming a citywide literacy initiative, which I will discuss later in the book.

I invite the reader to follow my journey as an academic librarian who loves to develop library programming; along the way I will introduce an array of programming ideas. Readers will find descriptions of some of my programs and those of other librarians from libraries big and small and of different types throughout the United States. Dozens of examples of successful programs that involve partnerships are shared. Readers who love library programming as much as I do will want to model or revise programs that they find here for use at their own institutions or with their own groups.

Promoting African American Writers: Library Partnerships for Outreach, Programming, and Literacy has six chapters with practical content. Here are descriptions of the chapters.

Chapter 1, "Working Together for Library Outreach: Promoting African American Writers," makes the case for inclusion, equity, and diversity in library programs and the promotion of African American authors. A starter list of names of African American writers and culture keepers from history and the twenty-first century is provided on which programs can be created. The list contains more than seventy writers and culture keepers—test yourself to discover how many of them you recognize. In Appendix A of the book, brief biographies are given for the persons named in the list. Chapter 1 outlines first steps to use in promoting the works of African American writers through programs for communities.

Chapter 2, "The National African American Read-In: A Model Program That Works," describes the literacy initiative referred to as the African American Read-In (AARI) that was founded by Jerrie Cobb Scott of the National Council of Teachers of English in 1989. Over the years, the AARI has attracted more than a million readers in the United States and in other countries. Chapter 2 highlights AARI programs that I've hosted. It also includes several case examples from other librarians who have hosted successful AARI programs in different parts of the United States.

Chapter 3, "Building Partnerships and Developing Programs That Promote African American Writers," is a guide to building partnerships. The purpose of forming partnerships, in my view, is to develop reciprocal relationships for the sponsorship of programs that are beneficial to the community and that help to meet the missions of libraries or other community organizations or groups. Types of library outreach programs that are based on partnerships are described using case examples of programs that promote African American writers and promote community-oriented service.

Chapter 4, "Identifying African American Writers for Programs," introduces different means of identifying African American writers for programs. For example, historical writing legacies of African American writers can be claimed through programs that are developed in partnerships with special collections of libraries or archives. Programs are described in which I and the Lilly Library at IU worked together to identify and celebrate African American writers for projects in partnership with each other. The chapter shows readers how to celebrate the historical African American writers who have a connection to their cities, states, or regions. Readers will be shown how programs may be planned by conducting an "in-reach" search to identify current, local African American writer talents within their own communities. Finally, means are shared that will help to identify new, nationally recognized African American writers. Numerous case examples of programs are provided.

Chapter 5, "Library Programming Assessment and African American Writer Programs," is an overview of types of assessments that may be conducted to evaluate library programs that have been designed around African American writers. It gives snapshots of some examples of assessments I've used in evaluating programs that I've coordinated or helped to sponsor to promote African American writers over the years.

Chapter 6, "Reflective and Intentional Programming to Promote African American Writers," gives practical advice to librarians, programmers, educators, and all those who work together to encourage the publishing and collecting of African American literature and writing. Librarians who lead programs must work to collaborate among organizations and inside organizations, interdepartmentally, with those who are responsible for collecting materials in libraries to encourage the collection of materials written by African American authors. Librarians can also take an advocacy role in favor of publishing more books by African American and other diverse writers. Given the roles of publishers and collectors of books in providing access to works by these writers, this chapter asks the question, What is the role that library programmers should play in "priming the pump" to keep a stream of published works by African American and other diverse writers going and easily accessible to use in programs? In this chapter, reflectivity and intentionality are analyzed as part of the programming process.

This book uses three overlapping concepts that are broadly applied: programing, promotion, and partnerships. The focus is on programs that feature African American writers, but I'm hopeful that the book will be helpful as a model for designing other programming as well. The Venn diagram displayed in this introduction illustrates how programming, promotion, and partnerships can take place separately, but the shaded portions of the diagram are intended to show that when these concepts coalesce, programs are more effective and lead to best practices. The center convergence in the diagram illustrates the goal that I hope this book encourages, which is that programs about African American writers are offered throughout whole communities and are optimally promoted and organized through collaborative partnerships.

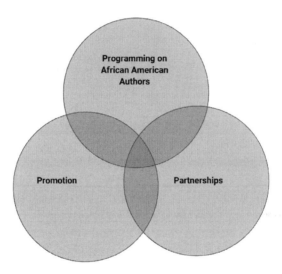

FIGURE I-1. Programming, Promotion, and Partnerships That Feature African American Writers

Working Together for Library Outreach: Promoting African American Writers

WORKING TOGETHER IN PROGRAMS THAT PROMOTE AFRICAN AMERICAN WRITERS

Libraries provide programs to connect with library users and potential users through activities that span the gamut from recreation to education. Library programming may involve everything from creating online tutorials for information resources to developing and hosting book clubs to organizing music concerts outside or inside the library walls. Libraries have always been viewed as cultural institutions, but in today's fast-paced, physical, and virtual world, libraries in the United States have become more competitive, even while maintaining their image as service institutions. Libraries are increasing their efforts to attract greater and greater numbers of visitors. Yet how much diversity is shown in their programming? Promoting African American writers through programming demonstrates diversity in libraries that can attract a wide range of new and loyal users to the library.

A Pew Research Center analysis of Census Bureau data (Fry and Parker, 2018) shows that "postmillennials" (persons six to twenty-one years of age) are the most racially and ethnically diverse part of the U.S. population with only a slight majority of them being non-Hispanic Whites (52 percent). African Americans as a whole, in 2019, were a relatively younger segment of the total U.S. population, according to a Pew Research Center report, with a median age of thirty-two (Tamir et al, 2021, 3). Many African Americans may be new library patrons who can be drawn into the library through promotion of African American writers. Evidence shows that providing African American youth with access to African American writers and literature increases their desire to read. An assistant professor in the School of Teaching and Learning at Illinois State University speaks on the importance of young students' eagerness to read and their engagement in reading when they see characters that look like themselves in books that are representative of their cultures, which improves their literacy skill.

> The students are more highly engaged. . . . Any child when they feel some connection to a book is going to be more into it, have more conversations around it—and then that leads to what we all want, which is greater gains when it comes to reading and critical thinking skills. (Collier, 2016, 14)

Two school librarians writing to make the case for inclusive multicultural collections in school libraries had this to say on the subject:

> We need books that illustrate the universality of life and the lives of people from different cultures. Books that show the sameness of various peoples show the richness of our differences. Books that reflect our own culture allow us to identify with those of other times or places, who have had experiences similar to ours. Books that reflect other cultures allow us to experience the lives of others with like problems. Each culture has a rich heritage, which may be seen through good literature, photographs, and illustrations. Through reading about other cultures, students will develop an appreciation for cultures and ethnicities other than their own. (Arsenault and Brown, 2007, 20)

It is important that librarians and others, through programming, work together to promote African American writers, which in turn will increase diversity education, motivate literacy, and encourage reading at all levels.

I will generally use the definition of a "program" that the National Impact of Library Public Programs Assessment (NILPPA) study uses. The latter study, conducted for the American Library Association (ALA) in 2017–2019, states that "a 'program' is an intentional service or event in a group setting developed proactively to meet the needs or interests of an anticipated target audience" (Barchas-Lichtenstein et al., 2019, 2). Therefore, I define "audience" as any library user(s) or potential library user(s). Exceptionally, however, I embrace library instruction as a possible form of library programs, while the NILPPA research study does not because all library instruction is not open to everyone in the general population. The NILPPA found that public libraries are the leader in sponsorship of library programs, followed by academic libraries, which sponsor a significant number of programs (ibid., 27).

Youth is an important population group that libraries want to attract, and more importantly must attract, as an audience for their organizations' programs as libraries build toward the future. According to a 2017 U.S. Census

Bureau Report, more than seventy-six million students were enrolled in U.S. schools nationwide from the kindergarten to college level (Census Bureau, 2018). Students are becoming a more diverse population, and library services must promote diversity and inclusion to attract these youth. Learning to develop outreach programs that promote African American writers can be useful as a model to develop other diversity outreach programs.

Libraries, through outreach, can connect with youth culture and with *whole communities*. However, there is no single definition for how libraries should connect with communities or conduct "outreach." Editors of one casebook on the subject assert that if you "ask ten different librarians to define it—and explain how they are doing it at their institutions—you will get ten different answers" (Sittler and Rogerson, 2018, vii).

One academic librarian defines library outreach as all "those efforts designed to engage users with library staff, services, or resources. It encompasses instruction, programming, committee and other collaborative work, and social media use" (Ramsey, 2016, 329).

Libraries provide outreach and programs to engage client populations of all ages and of all racial and ethnic groups within the immediate communities where they are located, as well as other physical and virtual communities for which they may have connections. *Promoting African American Writers* is a guidebook that provides program advice for accomplishing that.

ENCOURAGING READING, DIVERSITY, AND CULTURAL LITERACY

How do librarians and others promote African American writers in programs that provide forums for their work to be shared with the public for educational and cultural benefit?

Librarians can find inspiration and support from various advocates such as We Need Diverse Books (WNDB), an organization that emerged in 2014 from a grassroots group of children's book lovers using the hashtag #WeNeedDiverseBooks. A year later, in 2015, WNDB had become a trademark, nonprofit organization promoting diverse books, embracing the cultures of all children and youth. WNDB continues to grow and to expand its services. It is a rich, "go-to" resource for all programmers, writers, and publishers who want to promote diversity in literature, including Black writers. WNDB provides diverse resources for K–12 schools, gives different grant awards to young diverse writers, and partners with several book publishers that do similar promotional work.

African American literature is a unique part of American literature. African American writers emerged over hundreds of years to produce a rich literature. This literature originated in part from its roots in Africa and developed and thrived even after the enslavement of Africans in America. It often contains themes and storylines of struggles for freedom, human rights, and civil rights, as well as universal themes of love and sorrow. Enslaved Africans were forbidden even to speak their native languages. It was illegal to teach Africans and children born of Africans in America to read or write. Nonetheless, remnants of African culture survived through griots, music, and other oral communication traditions. People of African descent eventually learned to read and to write the English language. Over 400 years, despite racial barriers, an African American literature emerged and developed with poetry, novels, essays, plays, and other writings throughout the different periods of American history. Great African American writers can be found from the time of the antebellum South to Reconstruction, from the Great Northward Migration to the Harlem Renaissance, from the Civil Right Movement to urban protests, and from the Black Arts Movement to the twenty-first century. *Promoting African American Writers: Library Partnerships for Outreach, Programming, and Literacy* draws into the spotlight African American writers from many genres and specializations and from many time periods.

I use seven basic steps to develop much of the programming that I've organized and coordinated, or in which I've played a major role:

1. Decide on African American writer(s) to promote; focus on a program theme.
2. Recruit a working group to help generate ideas for the program.
3. Develop a timeline for program planning about twelve to eighteen months out.
4. Begin the work of completing the objectives of the program plan, including determining whether the writer(s) featured have their publications available in local libraries and bookstores or online.
5. Identify potential program partners from the local community within or outside an organization by doing a community analysis or environmental scan.
6. Recruit core individuals and/or organizations to become programming partners.
7. Continue "word-of-mouth" communication and networking, followed by program marketing.

GETTING STARTED WITH PROGRAM DEVELOPMENT

Step One: Decide on a particular writer or group of writers to promote. Then determine a program theme; or by deciding on a theme first, you may narrow the choice for a writer or writers. To provide inspiration of possible writers for programs I have some suggestions.

Here is a list of some genres and specializations along with names of some African American writers and culture keepers representative of those categories. I use the term "culture keepers" to refer to designates whose work is in whole or part representative of some categories such as storytelling, music lyricists, and rhyming that are traditions in the development of African American writing or expression that aren't recognized as formal writing. Each person named is listed in only one category, but some could be listed in multiple categories. Echo Brown, for example, might be listed as a story-teller, playwright, and nonfiction writer. Ta-Nehisi Coates might be listed as a journalist, novelist, and nonfiction writer. Eve L. Ewing might be listed as a nonfiction writer and a poet. The names provided here categorically list persons, living and deceased, for illustrative purposes only, as examples that programmers seeking to promote African American culture and writing may consider. A short biographical description for each person can be found in Appendix A of this book. There are many, many other writers who could be listed here. There are hundreds, even thousands, of African American persons who could be considered for programming.

- **African American children's book authors**: Kwame Alexander, Virginia Hamilton, Walter Dean Myers, Jason Reynolds, Mildred Taylor, Jacqueline Woodson
- **African American fiction writers**: Maya Angelou, James Baldwin, Octavia Butler, N. K. Jemisin, Toni Morrison, Colson Whitehead
- **African American film screenwriters/producers**: Julie Dash, Ava DuVernay, Spike Lee, Tyler Perry, John Singleton, Lena Waithe
- **African American storytellers and folktale writers**: Augusta Baker, Ashley Bryan, Echo Brown, Gladys Caines-Coggswell, Zora Neale Hurston, Jackie Torrence
- **African American graphic novelists, comic writers, and fantasy writers**: Bill Campbell, Ebony Flowers, Nnedi Okorafor, David F. Walker
- **African American hip-hop writers/spoken word and rappers**: Lauryn Hill, Kendrick Lamar, Queen Latifah, Gil Scott-Heron, Tupac Shakur, Saul Williams
- **African American journalists**: Robert Abbott, Ta-Nehisi Coates, Frederick Douglass, Charlayne Hunter-Gault, John H. Johnson, Ida B. Wells
- **African American nonfiction writers**: Angela Davis, Michael Eric Dyson, Henry Louis Gates Jr., Abrams X. Kendi, Cornel West, Isabel Wilkerson
- **African American orators, spokespersons, and speech writers**: Martin Luther King Jr., Lucy Terry Prince, Al Sharpton, Chuck Stone, Sojourner Truth, Malcolm X
- **African America poets**: Countee Cullen, Rita Dove, Eve L. Ewing, Nate Marshall, Tracy K. Smith, Natasha Trethewey
- **African American playwrights**: Jackie Sibblies Drury, Ed Bullins, Lorraine Hansberry, Lynn Nottage, Ntozake Shange, August Wilson
- **African American songwriters**: Nickolas Ashford and Valerie Simpson, James Cleveland, Thomas A. Dorsey, Dr. Dre, Holland-Dozier-Holland, Timbaland

Step Two: This involves recruiting a working group or committee to plan your program. During the pre–program planning stage, the planning group can help generate theme ideas for programs or, if a theme has already been decided on in Step One, how to implement the theme within the program. Invite into the discussion some persons who are demographically representative of segments of the audience that the library hopes to attract to the program. Bring into the discussion some library outsiders' perspectives. Holding brainstorming sessions on theme ideas may provide vital information about the wants and needs of both the library's regular patron base and potential new library users.

For example, in 2016, a coalition group named the Springfield African American Read-In (AARI), of which I was a part, chose the theme "African American Memories and Stories" for a Black History Month (BHM) celebration, anticipating that we could draw from a variety of writing and performance talents for a program or programs. The coalition group had prior success working with high school and middle school groups to perform African American poetry, spoken word, and choir music. The group had also developed a partnership with the Springfield Art Museum, which gave us free use of the museum auditorium with seating for about 400 persons. The "African American Memories and Stories" program attracted an audience of students, parents, teachers, and other interested community supporters that nearly filled the auditorium.

The Springfield AARI decided to hold a second program that year with a unique book discussion. Titled "A Visit with the Principals," it featured a panel of current and retired African American principals of the local public school system who were slated to share stories about their careers and to comment on the stories of two African American males who grew up in the 1990s in Baltimore, Maryland, as told in the book *The Other Wes Moore: One Name, Two Fates* by Wes Moore. The book, a *New York Times* bestseller, is based on a true story of the fate of two fatherless males born a few blocks from each other but whose lives took dramatically different turns— one becoming a Rhodes Scholar, a White House Fellow, and army officer, the other becoming a drug dealer involved in a robbery that resulted in a murder and a life sentence prison conviction. The book was also chosen as the "common reader" for the 2015–2016 freshman class at Missouri State University, a Springfield AARI organizational partner. The panel discussion was held on the campus of Drury University, also a Springfield AARI organizational partner. The panel was made up of four of the six principals who had led local Springfield public schools: Ferba Lofton (retired), Alana Lyles (retired), Nate Quinn (retired), and Nicole Holt (active). The panel was moderated by another African American public school leader—longtime mentor, teacher, and middle school counselor Gloria Morris. Following the panelist presentations, members of the audience actively asked the panelists questions.

However, despite our publicity efforts and hopes for a larger audience for the program from both the town and campus communities, only about twenty persons made up the audience, mostly from the communities around the college campuses. Perhaps interest on the college level, where the book *The Other Wes Moore* was required reading for incoming first-year students, had run its course. Perhaps "a visit with the principal" wasn't a theme that brought back favorite memories to many people. Our program organizers might have benefited from having focus groups or greater public input to test the attractiveness of the theme for this program. Still, we were able to attract a small and engaged audience. Audience attendance is an unpredictable factor in holding programming regardless of goal. Program developers should not become discouraged. Later in the book, I give some tips on increasing program audience participation as well as tips for programmer self-care and keeping up the morale of the program organizer team.

Topics for programs featuring African American writers may be matched to national BHM themes. A different theme is determined annually, often based on an anniversary in history or a current social–cultural topic decided on by the educators and historians of the Association for the Study of African American Life and History (ASALH). Consult the website of the ASALH to discover the annual theme for BHM and a listing of past ones (http://asalh.org/black-history-themes/).

The annual theme for BHM is published a year in advance by the ASALH journal *Black History Bulletin*, along with lesson plans and other supplemental information to plan for the observance. Negro History Week was founded in 1926 by historian Carter G. Woodson (1875–1950), who also founded the ASALH in 1915. The *Black History Bulletin* was started in 1937 at the urgings of educator Mary McLeod Bethune.

Woodson's vision was to bring recognition to the contributions of African Americans in the development of history in America and beyond. BHM began as Negro History Week to correspond with the birthdays of Frederick Douglass and Abraham Lincoln. In 1976, the commemoration was expanded to the full month of February. President Ford gave the first presidential proclamation for BHM, which became a standard practice of presidents who followed. In 1986, President Ronald Reagan delivered a proclamation encouraging the nationwide recognition of the contributions of African Americans during BHM in schools, libraries, colleges and universities, and other institutions in the United States.

I've developed programs around BHM subject themes for the BHM commemoration and to generally promote, year-round, the wide range of African American writers available and their writings. One such program was for BHM in 2014 in concert with the national BHM theme "Civil Rights in America." The program featured the first book of the graphic novel trilogy *March: Book One*, based on the life of civil rights leader and icon John Lewis and written by Lewis himself with coauthor Andrew Aydin. During the program, the Springfield AARI hosted a "virtual" interview between a group of high school students and the civil rights icon and Georgia congressman via Skype, a videoconferencing application. The program was planned in collaboration with high school instructors. Copies of *March: Book One* were distributed to students to read in preparation for the interview. In-class discussion time was scheduled, allowing students to take part in critical reflection and to prepare interview questions to ask Congressman Lewis.

Steps Three and Four establish a program timeline and set objectives. To develop your program to promote African American writers, establish a program planning timeline, ideally twelve to eighteen months out from the date that the actual program is to happen. Once a public program theme and/or purpose has been determined, develop the program around an anticipated audience's wants and needs. Planning should include objectives like determining arrangements for the featured writers, finding the best location or venue in which to hold the program, and reserving it based on the best dates and times to hold it.

Program planners must determine how to provide access to the writing represented by the theme. Determine whether books with the chosen theme and by the writer or writers are available to readers in local libraries, bookstores, and/or online. Are book signings and/or book sales wanted? Decide whether writer visits are desired as part of the public programming, because they may take a period of months to plan and organize. To schedule authors, the program planners must contact the writers or their publishers or agents to determine who is available for a specific program engagement date, and in some cases, to determine who might be affordable based on a programmer's budget. For budgeting, it's best to have selected two or three choices of guest writers as possible invitees in cases of glitches that may occur in matching your needs with that of writers.

Perhaps you and your working group of library program planners and other literacy partners do not want to feature an author visit, but rather want to develop other types of programs. There are many possible program options, including holding book club sessions, hosting a literacy program that features readers who read to children, sponsoring a summer reading program where an entire community choses one title and arranges book discussions around it, or having a program based around a poetry reading by readers or performers to highlight the work of one or more poets.

I manage coordination of programs by keeping a to-do list to make sure that tasks are completed according to deadlines, objectives are met, and programs are accomplished. Always delegate or obtain a volunteer to oversee each program task. Some program planners may choose to keep a record and progress report of program tasks by using a shared Excel spreadsheet or by using project management software. Burnout, or mental and physical exhaustion, is something the programmer should guard against. However, burnout is common among persons who are responsible for organizing events, especially mid-size to large-scale events. In my experience, burnout usually happens when one or two persons have responsibility for a disproportionate number of the tasks necessary for putting on a program or when someone is trying to "do it all" or "go solo." To avoid overworking any one individual, plan a fair division of the work that is needed for hosting the program. As the planning team moves forward through a planning timeline, make sure everyone on the team has a chance to celebrate small and large victories along the way, whether it be receiving a small monetary donation for the program or the signing of a contract by an author that has been recruited for the program.

Every program requires planning to implement it for best results.

IDENTIFYING LIBRARY PROGRAM PARTNERS IN LOCAL COMMUNITIES

Step Five in planning sponsorship of programs that promote African American writers is to identify potential program partners. How can librarians get to know their communities and discover the types of library programming that will be welcomed and enjoyed or that generates interest in African American writers? To start the process, identify potential program partners or community members who can provide invaluable input. Of course, one can always learn facts about a city or town where a library is located simply by reading through some of the census information and local government data. Official data is available for K–12 public schools and colleges and universities. One can also find official information about a local economy, such as its businesses and industries. But in my opinion, there is no substitute for getting out in person and exploring the physical and social terrain of one's community and talking with people. In addition, libraries and librarians can use social media to network with their communities. Regardless of method, it's always important to get out and meet and talk directly with people within communities.

There are many formal ways to conduct community analyses such as surveys, focus groups, and social media analytics. These formal ways may require staffing and are sometime expensive and/or time-consuming. Some persons of an organization or institution interested in doing programming may want to conduct what is called an "environmental scan." These formal means of learning about trends, opportunities, and threats affecting library communities are worthwhile and often necessary. Supplement the latter, however, with word-of-mouth communication and networking, which may be just as beneficial. "Coffee chats" with key leaders or representatives from the community and other informal conversations are a good option for finding out what's happening in the community and to discover persons or groups to partner with for programming.

Following are some ideas for developing partnerships with two vital contact groups: 1) students and other youth, and 2) civic and community leaders. Within the discussion of each category group for possible partnerships are embedded ideas for completing Steps Six and Seven: recruiting core individuals or organizations and continue networking followed by marketing.

Students and Youth

A key user group for all types of libraries is youth. Elementary and secondary teachers and school librarians need look no further than their own schools and school curriculum to begin a strategy for promoting African American writers and other diverse writers. School librarians who work closely with classroom teachers can develop reading lists of African American authors to support the school curriculum. They can develop makerspace projects and displays in the library to attract and motivate students to learn more about African American authors and other diverse authors. For example, librarians may assist students in finding an African American writer to read about by providing reading lists that are closely aligned to classroom curriculum. Students may do creative projects in makerspaces such as designing posters or bookmarks about a book author or a book title. School librarians and classroom teachers can collaborate with student learners to have groups of students or individual students make artistic items around a favorite book and, in the process, incorporate lessons for learning something about the African American author who wrote it. Posters can be displayed in the library or other places in schools such as the cafeteria. A contest for best poster or most creative artwork might be held and small prizes or recognitions be awarded.

Library programmers at any type of library (school, public, or academic) can build contacts with student organizations or youth groups (e.g., in Boys and Girls Clubs or in churches). These groups may agree to become partners with the library to accomplish programming goals. Student and youth organizations generally, if they "buy in" to library programs, bring enthusiasm and have networks that draw in audiences for programs and potential new library users. Try "top-down" and "bottom-up" approaches to make connections with instructors or advisors of youth organizations and clubs, as well as making direct contact with youth group leaders and group members. Attend events that youth organize and that are open to the public. Ask youth organization officers for an invitation to attend an organizational meeting to provide information about library services and programs and to ask for their input about possible future programs.

Furthermore, National School Library Standards position school librarians as learners alongside their student learners and school libraries as places of learning engagement. Collaboration is key in building these strong relationships among the library, the school librarians, classroom instructors, and students. It's more important than ever to include parents, and indeed whole communities, as partners with schools, which helps to build strong, healthy communities.

Partnerships between school librarians and public libraries have existed for decades and should be nurtured by programmers. Public libraries are a bridge for all youth in their growth to full citizenship and lifelong learning. Academic librarians can forge community service partnerships, too, with school libraries and public libraries to develop creative programming for outreach, diversity, and literacy. Librarians from all sectors and types of libraries in their community can work together to develop library programming with the goal of nurturing an appreciation for cultural diversity, intercultural communication, and lifelong learning.

Librarians at universities can build ties with academic departments by developing relationships with faculty members as library program cosponsors. Academic departments are often willing to cosponsor campus visits by scholarly writers, host a traveling exhibition, or try other programs. They are often open to sharing the costs of such programs. Academic librarians who serve as liaisons to academic departments should focus library programs on the teaching and learning that go on in the classroom and actively work to win the support of professors.

Librarians and educators at all levels can draw youth into libraries as an inviting place of learning, discovery, and fun by offering engaging programming.

Civic and Community Leaders

Identify "grassroots" community leaders as well as local civic leaders who may be supportive of and potential partners in your library programming. These leaders may be found in both the public and private sectors. They are individuals who may be found inside all levels of local government from the state level to the city where you live and work. Supporters may be found among small business owners, local managers of business franchises or companies, or in local churches or faith-based groups. Be optimistic and vigilant in seeking them out.

Attend local school board meetings and local government or civic organization meetings to learn of potential opportunities. Keep up with local news and current trends. Opportunities are all around and may emerge in surprising places. Through a city literacy program that promotes African American writers and literary I developed a one-year partnership with the local parks and recreation district that allowed free use of space in a community center for programs such as poetry reading/performances. A collaboration was developed with the Ozarks Storytelling Guild to offer a storytelling workshop for youth. An ongoing partnership was formed for programming support with the city's art museum, which provided an auditorium and other facilities for use gratis in support of our community outreach efforts.

While learning about the social and cultural terrain of your community, look for potential allies and partners who can help you to achieve your library programming goals. For the purposes of this book, allies are defined as those bringing short-term support such as one-time attendance to a program, while partners share long-term commitment to programming efforts and over time provide financial or in-kind support. Library programming partners share common goals and invest in making programs successful.

A group or a person may be a program contact who starts as an ally, such as a person who attends one library program event and posts a positive review about it to their social media contacts. But even a small relationship can potentially grow and develop into a partnership. A program leader is always looking for potential partners and works to build collaborative relationships.

Program marketing ideas will be discussed in Chapters 3 and 4.

FOLLOWING PROTOCOLS AND SOCIAL CAPITAL

In planning and coordinating library programming, there are two important areas to keep in mind: organizational protocol and social capital. To develop successful library programs, one must learn to follow protocols and to build and use social capital. Following protocols will help a library program leader to build bridges between library administration and one's program or project team, as well as to form bonds with organizational partners.

Social capital is both the tangible and intangible rapport that is important for program planners to possess. It enables one to navigate the terrains one encounters both inside and outside one's organization while planning and coordinating programs.

What Are Protocols?

Protocols are the rules and procedural guidelines that are followed within each organization and between organizations. Protocols vary by type of library—academic, public, school, and special. And protocols vary within each individual library organization. It's to your professional advantage, when developing and coordinating library programs, to be knowledgeable of the types and nuances of protocols involved. Understanding the protocols in one's organization is important to understanding the implementation of library programs and will pay dividends in carrying out your role as a library program planner!

Before venturing to build partnerships for programs, determine what partnerships your library already has. Talk to your supervisor to find out the library's guidelines or policies related to engaging in partnerships. Make sure you comply with them. Being informed about existing partnerships and projects will help you to determine whether others are involved in similar activities or programs before you start planning one. Can your program ideas be accomplished together with existing programs? Are they unique or different in a positive way? Are they worth pursuing independently, or should you try to partner with an existing program?

What Is Social Capital?

Librarians are service professionals, and libraries are mainly service institutions. Librarians and libraries both possess valuable services and goods that can be deemed social capital. Social scientists Adler and Kwon (2002, 17) define social capital as "the goodwill that is engendered by the fabric of social relations and that can be mobilized to facilitate actions." In the United States, librarians are mainly service professionals and libraries are primarily service institutions that exist for the public good, and both serve the communities where they are located. Librarians who are good program agents build social capital internally within their home organizations and outside their home organizations. Librarians who garner partnerships and solidify and broaden an audience base for programs are building social capital for their libraries. Librarians who build support for libraries in their communities are fostering or developing social capital for libraries as social institutions.

Universities are becoming more involved in their communities outside of their own institutional walls or campuses. Universities, particularly public universities that receive state and federal aid and tax dollars, are increasingly called on to provide outreach to the people in the cities and broader areas where they are located. Beginning in the 1990s, there was a strident effort to recognize early state legislative obligations that state universities have as "land-grant" institutions (Courtney, 2009, 4). Service learning and public affairs support was implemented by many institutions of higher learning nationwide during this period. Missouri State University, where I serve, became a Carnegie classified Community Engagement Institution.

The Carnegie Foundation for the Advancement of Teaching defines community engagement, generally, as the collaboration between institutions of higher education and their larger communities (local, regional/ state, national, global) for the mutually beneficial exchange of knowledge and resources in a context of partnership and development (nerche.org /defining-community-engagement/).

Promotion of African American writers and writing is an initiative of library outreach and literacy that builds working relationships among local universities, K–12 schools, public libraries, and civic groups, which reaps positive community outcomes such as encouragement of reading and increases positive diversity awareness and more intercultural group communication. These benefits can spread throughout the community.

University and college libraries' decreasing patron gate counts and declining circulation of collection items cause university administrators and academic librarians to consider alternative ways to increase the usage of college and university libraries. Various activities such as cultural and educational outreach programs to improve library use and public service projects to emphasize citizenship and community engagement are "tried-and-true" remedies. More academic libraries are participating in collaboration projects with a view toward building campus–community relations to increase public visibility, to bring more visitors into the university library, and to recruit students for college enrollment into their institutions.

SUMMARY

In this chapter, seven steps are suggested that library programmers may follow on their way to implementing successful programs. These steps will be expounded on further to provide a foundation for library programmers in general, and in particular those who have an interest in promoting African American writers for outreach, programming, and literacy.

A few words of advice are included in the chapter about following protocols when organizing programming. Final comments are made on the role that libraries have in garnering social capital and in providing social capital that helps to develop strong communities.

In the next chapter, the literacy initiative sponsored by the Black Caucus of the National Council of Teachers of English (NCTE) is highlighted. Founded more than thirty years ago, it's an ongoing program that's enjoyed yearly by readers in libraries, schools, private book clubs, community organizations, and by individuals across the United States and other countries engaging in reading works by African American writers. The Black Caucus of the NCTE, through their website, provides book lists, program promotional materials, and unifying means of communication so that hosts of the programs can learn what other read-in hosts have done in their programs and what other groups are reading. To illustrate what a read-in program involves, five case examples are provided in the next chapter. Read-in programs may be as elaborate or as simple as program hosts choose to make them.

REFERENCES

Adler, Paul S., and Seok-Woo Kwon. "Social Capital: Prospects for a New Concept." *Academy of Management Review* 27, no. 1 (January 2002): 17–40.
Arsenault, Rochelle, and Penny Brown. "The Case for Inclusive Multicultural Collections in the School Library." *CSLA Journal* 31, no. 1 (2007): 20–21.
Association for the Study of African American Life and History. "Black History Month Themes." http://asalh.org/black-history-themes/. Accessed March 17, 2019.

Barchas-Lichtenstein, J., R. Norlander, J. Voiklis, K. Nock, J. Fraser, and E. Danter. *National Impact of Library Public Programs Assessment: Summative Report.* NewKnowledge Publication #IML074.207.06. Chicago: America Library Association & New Knowledge Organization, June 2019.

Campus Compact. "Carnegie Community Engagement Classification." https://compact .org/initiatives/carnegie-community-engagement-classification/. Accessed April 2, 2019.

Census Bureau. "More Than 76 Million Students Enrolled in U.S. Schools, Census Bureau Reports." [News] Release Number CB18-192, December 11, 2018. https://www.census.gov/newsroom/press-releases/2018/school-enrollment .html. Accessed December 30, 2018.

Collier, Lorna. "No Longer Invisible: How Diverse Literature Helps Children Find Themselves in Books and Why It Matters." *The Council Chronicle* 26, no. 1 (September 2016): 13–17.

Courtney, Nancy. "Breaking Out of Our Shell: Expanding the Definition of Outreach in Academic Libraries." In *Academic Library Outreach: Beyond Campus Walls.* Edited by Nancy Courtney. Westport, CT: Libraries Unlimited, 2009.

Fry, Richard, and Kim Parker. "Early Benchmarks Show 'Post-Millennials' on Track to Be Most Diverse, Best-Educated Generation Yet." Pew Research Center, November 15, 2018. https://www.pewresearch.org/social-trends/2018/11/15 /early-benchmarks-show-post-millennials-on-track-to-be-most-diverse-best -educated-generation-yet/. Accessed January 5, 2022.

Lewis, John, and Andrew Aydin. *March: Book One.* Marietta, GA: Top Shelf Productions, 2013.

Moore, Wes. *The Other Wes Moore: One Name, Two Fates.* New York: Random House, 2011.

New England Higher Education. "Defining 'community engagement.'" Nerch.org /defining-community-engagement/. (Accessed June 15, 2022).

Ramsey, Elizabeth. "It's Not Just What You Know but Who You Know: Social Capital Theory and Academic Library Outreach." *College and Undergraduate Libraries* 23, no. 3 (2016): 328–334.

Sittler, Ryan L., and Terra J. Rogerson (Eds.). *The Library Outreach Casebook.* Chicago: Association of College and Research Libraries, 2018.

Tamir, Christine, Abbey Budiman, Luis Noe-Bustamante, and Lauren Mora. "Facts About the U.S. Black Population." Pew Research Center, March 25, 2021. https://www.pewresearch.org/social-trends/facts-about-the-us-black-popula- tion/. Accessed June 11, 2022.

2

The National African American Read-In: A Model Program That Works

In this chapter, we examine a sample of African American Read-In (AARI) programs and collaborative projects that originate from academic libraries. The national sponsor of AARI, the National Council of Teachers of English (NCTE), brings together programs that are hosted by all types of libraries and other civic and social organizations, as well as small groups of individuals such as private book clubs. One reason that the national AARI, which was founded more than thirty years ago, can be considered a model program is because of its broad appeal and flexibility. It can attract people of all ages and backgrounds. During its early years, the read-in was held in many school settings, prekindergarten through high school (pre-K–12). You will also find in this chapter AARI programs that are hosted by academic libraries. Some of these programs were sponsored by academic libraries in partnership with pre-K–12 schools.

The National AARI was founded in 1989. Over time, thousands have participated in its programs as the national AARI expanded its literary efforts with more services. Further background on the organization, including its founding and mission, is highlighted later in this chapter.

The read-in cases described in this chapter involved extensive planning; however, read-ins can be as simple or as elaborate as sponsors choose. Always design your programs around the wants and needs of your targeted audience and local communities.

In developing AARI programs in the Springfield, Missouri, community where I live and where the libraries are a major collaborative part of the initiative, I have discovered the following key benefits are achieved:

- Opportunities for community-based engagement
- New and experienced users drawn into the library

- Introduction of users to diverse materials and services in the library
- Promotion of reading and literacy

These are just some of the benefits that can be derived from the AARI and other programs that promote African American writers and other diverse writers. More advantages are described in the program examples provided in this and upcoming chapters.

NATIONAL AARI: AN OUTSTANDING AND LONG-RUNNING DIVERSITY LITERACY PROGRAM IN THE UNITED STATES

The African American Read-In (AARI) was founded by the late Jerrie Cobb Scott, a leader of both the Black Caucus and the general organizational body of the NCTE. Scott, a retired professor of urban literacy and former director of the Reading Center at the University of Memphis, died in 2017. Her vision for the AARI was to promote literacy and African American writers and to make reading an integral part of Black History Month commemorations and celebrations. In 1990, the whole NCTE organization adopted the AARI, helping to make it a national initiative (http://www.ncte.org/get-involved/african-american-read-in/). It is now likely one of the longest-running diversity literacy programs in the United States.

Scott (June 2, 1944–February 18, 2017) mentored many students and young teaching professionals throughout her life. In a published interview, on the twenty-fifth anniversary of the AARI, she stated,

> To get [young people] engaged, one of the things they need is to see themselves in books. They need to know some of the characters are African Americans just like some of them are. It is important for all of us to see ourselves in books, because that encourages us to read in a different way and encourages us to write more. (Aronson, 2014, 17)

The words in the quotation "It is important for all of us to see ourselves in books . . ." resonate with me as I write this guidebook and reflect on my own life and career. It is a phrase that every reader can relate to because seeing characters or persons in books that look like you or that you can relate to personally is likely to encourage you to read more. The joy of reading inspired me to achieve my goal of becoming a professional librarian!

The national AARI literacy initiative promotes its programs wherever readers can be found, including schools, faith-based institutions, libraries, and more. It originally encouraged readers to celebrate Black writers during

Black History Month. Since that time, the AARI caught the attention and imaginations of millions of readers in the United States and several other countries including the West Indies, Ghana, Germany, and Australia. Early in the organization's inception, it received endorsement by the International Federation on Reading. The AARI's ideals are celebrated and have expanded to promote the inclusion of reading of works by African American authors, not just in February but year-round.

Interested programmers can find the "National African American Read-In Toolkit" online through the NCTE/AARI website (http://www.ncte.org/get-involved/african-americanread-in-toolkit/). The toolkit contains suggestions for types of events to host, suggested works by African American authors, and even promotional materials to use for marketing read-in events.

The NCTE/AARI website encourages hosts of read-in events during February to complete an online "host report card" that registers the host city, state, organization name, and number of program attendees. I have found in hosting the Springfield AARI that it's helpful to designate someone to complete this report card to make certain that it's returned in a timely fashion. The AARI website has a blog that lets program hosts register their upcoming public events, allowing persons to learn about a variety of AARI programs across the country and to attend nearby programs. Since 1989, more than six million persons have been involved in the AARI.

The NCTE's pedagogical mission of literacy education views reading as a holistic process that teaches students to read, write, and think reflectively and critically (http://www.readwritethink.org). The NCTE Black Caucus embraces this philosophy, which carries over into their literacy programming and strategic planning. Each year, more persons of all ages, races, and ethnicities have participated in, learned from, and enjoyed AARI programs. Easy lesson plans are provided on the NCTE/AARI website to incorporate read-in ideas into the classroom.

AARI PROGRAM EXAMPLES

African American Read-Ins can take many forms and be planned for many types of audiences. For example, this chapter presents five contrasting AARI programs. Although three of the case examples describe celebrations with some reading of African American poetry, each is different. One of the programs targets a specific audience, while the other two are designed as open forums for the public. Storytellers and various types of readers are the highlight in one of the read-ins that is hosted for a general audience in a lunch setting. Another example, described here, features a virtual author visit and presentation by award-winning young adult author Brandy Colbert to a general audience at a public library.

EXAMPLE ONE: HIGH SCHOOL STUDENTS ON A UNIVERSITY CAMPUS

During the first decade of 2000, an assistant professor from Indiana University (IU) on the main campus in Bloomington and in the School of Education, Stephanie Power-Carter, introduced the African American Read-In literacy initiative to Indiana University-Bloomington (IUB), which embraced the idea. I first learned about the AARI while I served as a librarian at IUB. Power-Carter, a member of NCTE and at the time a new IU assistant professor, annually coordinated visits to the IU campus by hundreds of local area high school students, mostly African Americans, to participate in AARI programs. These visits involved working with local high school administrators and teachers to arrange the nearly daylong field trips that required time away from regular classes and school bus transportation.

IUB is the main campus of the three satellite locations of the large research university. Its campus is a beautiful, sprawling two thousand acres located in the midwestern town. Bloomington is about an hour and a half drive from Indianapolis. In 2007–2008, IUB had a student enrollment of about 27,000. During the academic year 2020–2021, IU student enrollment had grown to more than 42,500.

For many of the high school students who visited the IUB campus for the AARI from local communities, it was likely a first-time visit to the campus. The students always appeared to be excited about the gatherings. Faculty member Power-Carter and other university instructors and students held the high school students' attention and engaged them with poetry written by African American poets. Students and teachers met in a ballroom-size space inside the university's Neal-Marshall Black Culture Center (NMBCC). Students performed or read aloud poems by African American poets, as well as their own original works, to an audience mainly of their peers.

In a scholarly journal article published about her work with high school students and the AARI, Power-Carter states:

> [M]ost of the original writing students share at the African American Read-In deal with the challenges that they face as Black youth grappling with topics such as Black manhood, Black female stereotypes, Black family, skin color, and what it feels like to be bi-racial. Research has shown that identity affirmation is central to school success for some Black youth (e.g., Delpit; Freeman; Harris, Kahmi, and Pollock; Ladson-Billings; Taylor). The African American Read-In is an important opportunity for schools to celebrate and acknowledge Black writers as well as create culturally affirming spaces. (Power-Carter, 2007, 23)

The high school students attending the AARI forums were treated to a memorable experience on the IUB campus. They were immersed in the art of African American poetry and writings with the fellowship of their peers while standing alongside mentors from the IU faculty, staff, and students. Other educational and recreation activities were provided during the day, as was lunch. The occasion was a great learning experience and energy booster for the high school student visitors.

EXAMPLE TWO: PUBLIC READING EVENTS AT A UNIVERSITY

University of Missouri-Kansas City (UMKC) is a large comprehensive university of about sixteen thousand students situated in a metropolitan area. It offers a wide selection of undergraduate academic majors to its students, in addition to a medical school and other graduate programs. It is a satellite institution of the main campus that is located in Columbia.

Gloria Tibbs was a university librarian at UMKC; I met her while doing research on AARI programs in the state of Missouri. Tibbs and I would later cowrite and publish a journal article about our involvement with AARI projects. She had a unique, energizing approach to the AARI programs that she led. She coordinated these programs at UMKC for many years, but each time she brought something slightly different to the event.

Tibbs coordinated an annual AARI at her university that involved volunteers of students, faculty, staff members and other affiliates. She brought these groups together to organize public reading events. Persons were requested to register in advance to read aloud a favorite selection from an African American author such as an excerpt from a novel or a play, a poem, or a song. During the read-in events, which were open to the public on the UMKC campus, traditional African American desserts such as homemade peach cobbler, red velvet cake, and a read-in organizer original—"sweet potato pie cookies"—were served as refreshments at the event. The foyer of the university library, which was a large open space, served as the venue for the read-in events.

Tibbs stated that the refreshments that are provided each year have a theme "tie-in" that helped to bond people together. During the read-in, audience members enjoyed the desserts along with the entertaining literary readings and performances. The audience members engaged informally with each other in a pleasant, relaxing environment. She stated this about the AARI events that she organized:

> Personalization . . . includes complimentary refreshments for the UMKC AARI event. . . . While enjoying refreshment tie-ins to the vibrant and rich cultural AARI, conversations flow and connections are made. (Jackson-Brown and Tibbs, 2013, 365)

Even after her retirement, persons at UMKC continued to celebrate the AARI traditions that she started more than a decade earlier.

EXAMPLE THREE: A COLLABORATIVE PARTNERSHIP

In Springfield, Missouri, as a library faculty member at Missouri State University (MSU), I was the participant/project leader of a collaborative partnership, the Springfield African American Read-In (AARI). This partnership was founded in 2009–2010. I recruited a steering committee made up of at least one representative from each of the five partnering organizations, which were MSU, Drury University, the Springfield-Greene County Library District, the Springfield Public Schools, and the Springfield chapter of the NAACP. Each year, steering committee members recruited students, teachers, staff, and others from their respective institutions and affiliations to volunteer to do the work necessary for AARI programs.

The team of volunteers through their deeds show commitment to the ideals of the citywide AARI. Their duties run the gamut in many different areas, including assisting in rehearsals for programs; creating, copying, and distributing flyers; providing publicity through social media and traditional media; setup and cleanup for programs; and sending thank-you messages after the programs. Contributions, big or small, are important and appreciated.

MSU, where I have served as a university librarian for more than fifteen years, has a public affairs mission. Through teaching, learning, and service, MSU educates persons using the three "pillar" themes of ethical leadership, cultural competence, and community engagement as part of its public affairs mission. In accordance with the university's mission, I received support in leading the AARI literacy and diversity outreach initiative. In the beginning years of the Springfield AARI, MSU was a comprehensive university with a student enrollment of about twenty-three thousand. Over the years, MSU through strategic planning grew and expanded, reaching its goal of becoming a research institution by adding more graduate programs and increasing its student enrollment to about twenty-six thousand in 2019–2020.

Publicity or marketing for the Springfield AARI contains the logos of the five organizations that make up the collaborative partnership. Each partnering organization contributes monetary and/or in-kind support. From the beginning, the Springfield AARI was a prime example of a "town and gown" partnership, that is, a collaborative relationship between a university and local town or city. In the case of the Springfield AARI, it operates with two academic institutions, Missouri State University and Drury University, and community ties with three local entities.

In 2011, I delivered a conference paper for the Association for College and Research Libraries published in their conference proceedings, which describes publicity and other work for the inaugural Springfield events that took place in the fall of 2009 and a finale in February 2010.

> [A] Facebook fan page was started. One of the MSU partner offices, the Office of Multicultural Programming & Student Diversity, provided college student volunteers to assist with registration tables at pre-events.
>
> During the two-day AARI celebration in February 2010, events were held at various locations throughout the city. One of the AARI committee members, MSU education professor Sabrina Brinson, led some of her students in providing an interactive story time for children and persons of all ages. One of the larger public libraries served as the host for the finale AARI Poetry Reading Performance that featured stage presenters from high schools, colleges, and community adult mentors.
>
> Approximately 90 persons, primarily local community children and youth, participated in the two pre-events of the AARI literacy project: a Young Writers Workshop for middle school youth led by award-winning author Patricia McKissack on October 17, 2009, and a storytelling session and book signing by master storyteller and new author Gladys Caines-Coggswell on November 15, 2009. Attendance at the finale on February 21 and February 22, 2010 numbered more than 350 persons. (Jackson-Brown, 2011)

Following the AARI finale, a front-page newspaper article reflected the event's impact on audience participants by its headline title, "Rhythm in the Words, with Meter and Volume, with Humor and Sorrow, African-American Poetry Draws a Diverse Crowd," and its one-sentence lead paragraph, "There may have been one or two seats left open at Monday night's African American poetry reading at the Springfield Library Center—but just one or two" (Wall, 2010, 1).

More information is provided about inaugural Springfield AARI events in later chapters.

EXAMPLE FOUR: A COMBINED CAMPUS AND COMMUNITY EVENT

This chapter highlights a case example written by academic librarian Michelle E. Jones from Columbus State University in Columbus, Georgia. Columbus State is a liberal arts university with a student enrollment of about eight thousand. It is ranked among the top regional universities in the South by *U.S. News and World Report*. Its 132-acre campus is located within the city of Columbus.

Jones has led, for more than ten years, a combined campus and community AARI event at the school. The event, which has grown and expanded over the years, includes both professional and layperson participation, as well as faculty and students. According to this case example, the coordinated work of putting forth the programs is the result of broad collaborative efforts.

CSU LIBRARIES AND THE AFRICAN AMERICAN READ-IN: EXPANDING OUR IMPACT

By Michelle E. Jones

I have had the privilege of coordinating the African American Read-In at Columbus State University (Columbus, GA) for the past nine years. My primary method of working on this event has been to create a partnership through departments at the university or in the community. Though I am not completely sure when the first read-in was held at Columbus State, my history with the event began in 2010 with a now retired colleague. During her tenure at the university, she coordinated the event and invited me to assist her.

Our initial grassroots programming centered on asking university staff, students, and faculty to read from their favorite African American–authored work during timed presentations. Lunch was provided for audience members. This involved advertising the event far in advance to allow potential readers to sign up with title/author and to prepare a presentation. A library colleague with a background in art graciously designed our event poster for many years. Many who signed up were grateful for the opportunity. Most of the readers were faculty members, with a few students included.

The highlight of the event took the form of a professional storyteller. These talented artists were usually based in Georgia. Some of the storytellers would give the university a reduced rate. One asked to be linked to local public schools so that she could offer her skills at more than one venue. Additionally, this storyteller performed at an elementary school and a high school. That was a wonderful collaboration, enabling the school district to receive discounts and high-caliber talent because of multiple engagements in the same city on consecutive dates.

In another year of the event, we partnered with the English Honor Society, Sigma Tau Delta. That year an alumna/local actress was the highlight of the event instead of a professional storyteller. Every year following, people began to look forward to the actress's performance because her talent was exemplary. University students, staff, and faculty were still highly encouraged to sign up to participate to read as in previous years. However, we noticed that it was becoming more difficult to get university participation. There was plenty of interest in attending, but we needed to somehow reinvigorate speakers or readers.

The planning then morphed from primarily using university staff, students, and faculty to focusing more on bringing the community to the university venue. We worked with an English professor to help with advertising. This boosted our profile because the poster now appealed to more people since the faculty worked with an online company to publish it. This was our first year specifically targeting individual speakers from the community. Due to the community affiliations of this professor, we were able to bring in some high-profile local people along with one or two university faculty and students as readers. An emcee other than the event coordinator was also introduced. Such a strategy was a magnificent success, with attendance surpassing all other years.

In a following year, I began to work with a different English professor. Her vision involved coming up with a theme for the read-in. Our advertising continued to stay on par with previous years as we worked with a graphic designer for the poster. Again, we chose specific people to invite as participants. Audience involvement was distinctive, as many became engrossed in the discussion deriving from the speakers' presentations. One year, the event was broadcast on the local television news. By this time, we knew to prepare lunch and space for a crowd of at least fifty or more. The event was becoming a revered one that many anticipated each year.

In short, we have found a method that works for the read-in. The library added an outreach librarian to the staff who can help with the promotion and food for the event. Now, all I must do is concentrate on the content. The event was featured in the local newspaper. Over the years we have discussed and read from the writings of various African American authors—some known and many unknown. Speakers find their own unique voice when preparing for the event because of the author and work chosen. Audience members are also enlightened to glean from the experience. It is my sincere hope that we continue to offer this event for many more years to come.

Michelle E. Jones is head of reference services and associate professor of library science, Columbia State University, Columbus, GA.

EXAMPLE FIVE: VIRTUAL EVENTS

As the United States and the world fought against the spread of the COVID-19 pandemic in 2020 and 2021 and into 2022, American libraries found a way to continue to offer programs for community engagement, learning, and leisure. Programs include digital story times, book club gatherings via Zoom or other internet platforms, and hosting of virtual author visits. The Springfield AARI, through its partnerships with the Springfield Public Schools, the Springfield-Greene County Public Library District, and its other partners, provided its thirteenth read-in event in 2022, with precautionary measures. A program featuring retired Springfield educator and children's book author Charlotte Cosby was held in a venue where appropriate social distancing was practiced by the audience. Using a Zoom format, Cosby gave her presentation on her children's book *Dad's Mission: A Pictorial History of Colonel Frederick Drew Gregory, U.S. Astronaut*. In a second program, we hosted award-winning young adult author and Springfield native Brandy Colbert in a virtual Zoom presentation. Following the presentation, students and others asked "live" audience questions in an interview format.

Colbert first received critical accolades in 2014, when her debut novel *Pointe* was given a starred review from *Publishers Weekly* (Burlington et al., 22). Her second novel, *Little & Lion* (2017), received the 2018 Stonewall Children's and Young Adult Literature Award. Following this, Colbert published other works, including young adult novel *The Voting Booth* (2020). In 2021, she published a nonfiction book, *Black Birds in the Sky*, that recounts the historical facts of the Tulsa Race Massacre in a style suitable for young adults to read and learn about this horrible act of racial terrorism that happened in America.

Colbert teaches courses on writing children's and young adult literature at Hamlin University in St. Paul, Minnesota.

SUMMARY AND SUGGESTED AARI PROGRAM FORMATS

In summary, AARI programs vary in design. In this chapter, five exciting programs with different formats for reading inspiration are shared from four universities. At the end of this summary, a list of suggested formats for the AARI and other programs is provided.

Sometimes, partnerships that programmers build may influence the formats that programs take. For example, programmers may build a partnership with a Black repertory theatre group in their city or at the university where they're based and develop collaborations with them for play productions.

Below is a list of possible formats to use when planning AARI programs or other programs to promote African American writers.

Book Talks
Children's Story Times
Panels, such as Speakers on Diverse Literature
Exhibits
Writing Workshops
Storytelling
Author Visits
Book Illustrator Visits
Poetry Slam Competitions

Poetry Readings and Spoken Word Performance
Film Screenings tied to Book Title(s) and Discussions
Book Clubs
Performance of a Play or a Skit
Writers' Showcase or Festival of local authors, university faculty members, etc.

REFERENCES

Aronson, Deb. "The African American Read-In Marks 25 Years by Looking Forward." *The Council Chronicle* 24, no. 2 (November 2014): 17–18.

Burling, Alexis, Nathalie Op De Beeck, Samantha Henderson, Michael Levy, Sue Corbett, and Donna Freitas. "Spring 2014 Flying Starts." *Publishers Weekly* 261, no. 26 (2014): 17–22.

Colbert, Brandy. *Black Birds in the Sky: The Story and Legacy of the 1921 Tulsa Race Massacre*. New York, NY: HarperCollins Publisher, 2021.

Colbert, Brandy. *The Voting Booth*. Los Angeles, CA; Hyperion, 2020.

Colbert, Brandy. *Little & Lion*. New York, NY: Little, Brown and Company, 2017.

Colbert, Brandy. *Pointe*. New York, NY: G. P. Putnam's Sons, 2014.

Cosby, Charlotte. *Dad's Mission: A Pictorial Biography of Colonel Frederick Drew Gregory, U.S. Astronaut*. United States: In Writing Publications, 2020.

Jackson-Brown, Grace. "Building a 'Town and Gown,' Collaborative Partnership to Promote Diversity and Literacy: A University Library's Involvement in the National African American Read-In Chain Literacy Initiative." Paper Presented at the ACRL 2011 Conference, *A Declaration of Interdependence*, Philadelphia, March 30–April 2, 2011. https://www.ala.org/acrl/sites/ala.org.acrl/files/content/conferences/confsandpreconfs/national/2011/papers/building_collaborati.pdf. Accessed June 5, 2022.

Jackson-Brown, Grace, and Gloria Tibbs. "The African Read-In: Building Campus-Community Partnerships." *College and Research Libraries News* 74, no. 7 (July 2013): 364–367.

Power-Carter, Stephanie. "The African American Read-In: Celebrating Black Writers and Supporting Youth." *English Journal* 96, no. 4 (March 2007): 22–23.

Wall, Kathryn. "Rhythm in the Words." *The News-Leader*, February 23, 2010: 1.

3

Building Partnerships and Developing Programs That Promote African American Writers

PARTNERSHIP PLANNING FOUNDATIONS

In this chapter, I share some of my experiences in developing program partnerships in the African American Read-In (AARI) and other library programs. I share successes as well as challenges in hopes that readers might find valuable takeaways that are useful to them in building their own program partnerships. In addition, this chapter includes case examples from other programmers who are involved in building partnerships for programming in the areas of outreach, diversity, and literacy. Readers will find useful, practical tips for forming relationships and working together. To begin, here is a list of key steps that I use in building a strong foundation for successful collaborations or partnerships.

- Have a project leader who's in charge of coordination and communication.
- Begin by setting project goals and objectives.
- Have a steering committee whose members can each be responsible for key tasks and recruit volunteer helpers.
- Decide early how resources (people, time, money) will be pooled.

Some partnerships work very well informally, while others operate better with a formal structure, such as those drawn up in written "Articles of Agreement" that guide them in carrying out their activities. Both arrangements can be productive, depending on the circumstance. Articles of Agreement are often used in businesses and guide such things as purpose of the entity, voting rights, and management rules or guidelines. The Springfield

AARI works well as an informal, collegial group that makes decisions by consensus.

Regarding keys to success in partnerships, the most important is having a clearly defined purpose that is agreed on by members of the partnership. The purpose of the Springfield AARI is twofold: 1) promote African American writers, and 2) build a community of lifelong readers. Our purpose is documented on our printed pamphlets, on our website, and in other communications. It is referenced in all official publications about the organization and frequently announced during our programs. Periodically, we review our purpose to ensure that we are staying on track with our mission.

A tool that partnerships that are nonprofit organizations or charitable groups often have is 501(c)3 status to assist them in accomplishing goals. Nonprofits apply through the federal revenue service for 501(c)3 status. This status gives nonprofit organizations federal tax exemption. It allows them to accept donations from individuals, which are then tax-deductible. The 501(c)3 status is often required in applications for government and other types of grants.

The Springfield AARI, as a group, does not have 501(c)(3) status. The individual organizations that make up the partnership consortium that do have this special tax-exempt status sometimes apply for grants on behalf of the whole AARI. The Springfield AARI has no firm, guaranteed budget from year to year, but relies on charitable donations and on each organizational partner to annually pool monies to cover programming and other expenses.

Each organizational partner of the Springfield AARI provides one or two representatives to serve on a steering committee for the organization as a body. In addition, at least one volunteer person is selected from the community at-large to serve on the steering committee. Each year, steering committee members serve as leaders in the recruitment of volunteers to help carry out programming and other activities for the AARI.

POINTERS FOR DEVELOPING K–16 PARTNERSHIPS

Where does one start to build K–16 (kindergarten through senior year of college) school partnerships, especially if one is an outsider or not directly part of a K–12 public school system?

Networking and joining resources with K–12 public schools is beneficial to accomplishing shared goals such as encouraging literacy. In building partnerships with public schools, one may find allies with teachers, school librarians, principals, and parent–teacher organizations. When a school librarian or teacher seeks project collaboration, for example, with a nonprofit literacy organization, that relationship is sometimes called an "inside-out" approach because those with formal ties to the schools are the ones reaching out to external allies. Having internal ties with K–12 schools makes working together easier for outside groups because school insiders are knowledgeable about opportunities for programming areas to support elementary and secondary school curricula or for valuable extracurricular activities that support different schools' missions.

When school librarians take the lead in reaching out to programmers in nearby universities, this often makes for a successful partnership. In a case example in this chapter, school librarian Erika Long describes a collaborative relationship that she developed with university instructors to provide opportunities for her students to take part in an African American Read-In celebration hosted by the University of Tennessee in Knoxville. She also describes establishing a partnership with a classroom instructor at her school to develop a curriculum lesson plan that included a school visit by an African American author.

PROMOTING BLACK WRITERS IN SCHOOL LIBRARIES

By Erika Long

Diversity in literature is a theme we often hear discussed in librarianship. It's an even more relevant topic among school librarians and other educators. Our goal is always to provide our students with literature that reflects not only the community they live in, but a global perspective as well. Students deserve and need literature that reflects their lives and allows them to experience the lives of others.

One of the most prominent ways school librarians promote Black authors and diversity in literature is through collection development—the thoughtful and intentional selection of materials by Black and other writers of color (and other underrepresented groups). By doing so, we implement the Include Shared Foundation of our National School Library Standards—establishing a collection that supports a range of learners. While achieving the goal of a diverse collection is important, it is only a start.

Working in secondary libraries has afforded me the opportunity to go a step further. I previously worked in a high school that was closely connected to our state's largest university, University of Tennessee in Knoxville. Each year, the Center for Children's and Young Adult Literature (CCYAL) at the university hosts an African American Read-In during the month of February. Although the event was held during school hours, through collaborative efforts between teachers and the CCYAL, students were empowered to participate in the read-in by submitting videos of themselves reading from works by Black writers to be downloading during the event. Yes, this was exposure to authors they knew, but even more, works they weren't familiar with. Through participating in the read-in, students' reading participation and knowledge of Black authors expanded beyond their required reading.

Another opportunity to take advantage of, when available, is inviting authors to your school. Recently, I hosted my first author visit at my school. Of course, when hosting an author visit, it is essential that students are familiar with an author's work. The eighth-graders who attended had the experience of a lifetime. Their humanities teacher and I collaborated to incorporate *Pride* into their curriculum. Using this remix of *Pride and Prejudice* as a novel study for English and its inclusion of gentrification for social studies was the perfect opportunity to invite YA author Ibi Zoboi to speak. Not only did students at my school—whose population is majority Black—have the chance to hear an author who is of a similar background, they engaged with someone whose physical and literary neighborhoods reflected their own community. Having this unique experience served as a catalyst for students designing a community for their project-based learning.

I'm challenged even more now to bring more experiences with Black authors and literature to my students.

Erika Long is a school librarian in Tennessee.

In addition to partnering with nearby universities, K–12 classes and library programmers with an interest in promoting African American writers may partner with local civic or social groups such as NAACP chapters, Black fraternities and sororities, and Black churches. These are all potential collaborators that have an interest in developing community service projects such as assisting with literacy programs.

In another case example shared here, Professor Shurita Thomas-Tate describes her work in building a partnership that supports literacy needs of the community while at the same time providing her university students, who are studying communication science and disorders, a valuable service-learning experience.

UJIMA PARTNERSHIPS

By Shurita Thomas-Tate, PhD, CCC-SLP

Our nonprofit organization is Ujima Language and Literacy (Ujima). Ujima is a Swahili word that means "collective work and responsibility." It is one of the seven principles of Kwanzaa (an empowering, nonreligious cultural observation) that is the guiding belief for our programming that broadly focuses on school readiness, grade-level reading attainment, family engagement, and cultural consciousness. Founded by Dr. Shurita Thomas-Tate, Ujima was initially conceived during the fall of 2015 as an opportunity for her to provide a service to the community and an opportunity for her students to develop cultural consciousness skills in language and literacy. Five organizations—Missouri State University Department of Communication Sciences and Disorders, NAACP-Springfield Branch, Bartley Decatur Neighborhood Center, Springfield-Greene County Library District, and Springfield Public Schools—were brought together in early 2016 to formalize Ujima Language and Literacy. Since our inception, our partnerships have grown to include local churches, banks, and numerous community groups. Ujima partners (which include the families being served) work together in a multifaceted, holistic model to create long-term community change and commitment. We currently have two strands of programming.

Ujima Summer Literacy Camp. This program is designed to prepare students for kindergarten, support elementary students needing extra help in reading, and provide literacy and language enrichment to combat loss of skills during the summer. Students are engaged in small-group instructional interventions focusing on core reading skills (e.g., phonological awareness, vocabulary, and oral language comprehension and fluency) during the first half of the day. Literacy instruction/intervention is embedded in a variety of games and activities that is implemented by Missouri State University graduate students from the Department of Communication Sciences and Disorders. The graduate students are supervised by a licensed speech-language pathologist and receive clinical clock hours toward the completion of their degree. Additional learning opportunities, as well as field trips, art, music, fun, and games, take place during the second half of the day. Community partners and community volunteers staff the camp. Ujima Summer Literacy Camp receives operations support through generous monetary and in-kind donations for facilities, food, books/materials, and staffing of the camp.

Ujima Family Literacy Nights. These are monthly gatherings for the whole family, designed to partner with parents to encourage the love of books and reading, and to engage kids in fun, age-appropriate language and literacy activities. We start our evening with dinner and opportunities for dinner conversation. After dinner, children are grouped by age to read books and play games. At the end of the night, every child selects a book to take home from a specially curated collection of books representing cultural diversity. Like our summer camp, community partners and community volunteers fund and staff our Literacy Nights.

We can accomplish more for our community when we work together. Each partner brings specialized talents and strengths to accomplish a common goal. In the case of Ujima Language and Literacy, the common goal is increasing literacy and strengthening families within a cultural conscience frame. Our K–12 students and families gain the strength of community and social capital to navigate a challenging educational scene. My MSU students are embedded in a culturally and linguistically diverse setting that allows them to develop and apply skills beyond the university classroom. My community partners make it all happen. While each of my partners may come to Ujima with their own needs and goals, our shared vision for the Ujima families is what matters most.

Shurita Thomas-Tate, PhD, CCC-SLP, is an associate professor at Missouri State University and the founder of Ujima Language & Literacy.

One may find support from a university or school district through a "chief diversity officer" to help develop partnership efforts. Most educational institutions have strategic plans or missions that are committed to diversity, and one of the main job responsibilities of a chief diversity officer or other similarly named official is to take a leadership role in implementing activities to support this area. Librarians and other programmers should strive to "get a seat at the table" of relevant decision-making bodies or boards to present the case for partnership programs like the ones that the Springfield AARI offers to promote African American literature and writers and to build lifelong learners. Literacy programs are useful to promote diversity and build cultural competence among youth. These programs are a healthy mechanism to open lines of intercultural communication. In my experiences I've made the case for the former in literacy programming many times and have come to view advocacy as a part of my role in developing partnerships that promote African American writers and diverse literature.

SERENDIPITY IN THE EVOLUTION OF A TEN-YEAR PARTNERSHIP

It's important to determine appropriate protocols and reliable contacts to build a working partnership with a school system. This will help programmers seeking to form partnerships to move forward in an efficient, effective, and responsible manner. Guidelines for forming partnerships with public schools will likely be different in each school or school district. And, depending on the size of a school district, the responsibility for it might be with a curriculum coordinator, diversity officer, or a development officer. When one is not employed by a school system and tries to build a partnership with a school or schools, this is called an "outside-in" initiative. I learned early on that the former is often very difficult, if not impossible, to accomplish.

I had moved to Springfield, Missouri, in 2008. I was a newcomer to the city when I decided to proactively take the lead to develop a partnership to introduce the African American Read-In literacy initiative to the public schools. There were numerous obstacles that I had to overcome. I was not knowledgeable about SPS, which at that time was the second-largest school system in the state of Missouri. I had never taught in a public school or any K–12 learning environment. I had never worked as a school librarian. I had spent most of my career in academic libraries with a few years of experience in a public library. I learned by serendipity how to navigate and develop a partnership with SPS. I engaged in numerous communications and consultations to learn how to take the first step to receiving cooperation in publicizing a major Springfield AARI event, a workshop to be led by well-known and well-respected children's author Patricia McKissack. It was recommended that I contact the SPS language arts coordinator and work through her to distribute publicity about the workshop.

I contacted the coordinator to request that she facilitate having a flyer about the AARI event added to the teachers' pre-academic-year service packet during that summer. The flyer was quickly composed and created. It wasn't the highest-quality publicity, but it did contain all the basic information that the AARI committee needed to distribute about the AARI event that was scheduled in the month of October.

This rocky start for the Springfield AARI became smoother with time and led to a successful, long-term partnership between the Springfield AARI and SPS. The programs described in this chapter are not in chronological order but represent different periods in my professional growth and the growth of the literacy programs that I've helped to lead.

Fast-forward to the ten-year anniversary of the Springfield AARI, and I am serving as its chairperson and have found an individual from within SPS who shared the literacy and diversity goals of the organization—Marty Moore, the executive director of Learning Support and Partnerships of SPS. After I connected with Moore, the AARI steering committee and SPS worked together to schedule the showing of a traveling exhibition, *Telling a Peoples' Story: African American Children's Illustrated Literature*, along with hosting presentations by the *New York Times* best-selling children's book illustrator AG Ford.

Telling a People's Story: African American Children's Illustrated Literature was a first-of-its-kind art exhibition, showcasing original art of African American book illustrators that was used to tell the story of African American culture and history through the pages of children's books. The exhibition was first held at the Miami University Art Museum in Oxford, Ohio, from January 30, 2018, through June 30, 2018. A past librarian employee of the Miami University, King Library, I learned of the exhibition during a return visit to Oxford. The exhibition was created by Jason E. Shaiman, curator of exhibitions at the Miami University Museum of Art. The exhibition consisted of original art from the children's books with an accompanying symposium that was well received by scholars and the general public. It was reformatted digitally into panels to create a smaller, traveling version with the help of grant support from the Martha Holden Jennings Foundation.

The Springfield AARI showed the exhibit at two locations in the city, a branch public library named the Library Center and the Duane G. Meyer Library on the Missouri State University (MSU) campus. The opening reception of the exhibit and the Tenth Anniversary Springfield AARI celebration was held at the Library Center with music, song, and poetry readings for an audience of about 170 adults and children. Congratulatory remarks were delivered by Marty Moore, the SPS executive director of Learning Support and Partnerships and Regina Greer Cooper, the executive director of the Springfield-Greene County Library District. Soon after the exhibit opening, a parent mailed a handwritten note to the library, which said, "Thank you, African American Read-In Group, for 'Telling a People's Story' Exhibit. Truly a Gift to Share a True Story," signed "Appreciative Concerned Mom." In this chapter, readers will find the publicity flyer used during the tenth anniversary celebration (see Figure 3-3).

When the exhibit was shown on the MSU campus, a student reporter wrote a feature article for the campus student newspaper, *The Standard* (Harper, 2019, 10). The article carried an interview with Jason Shaiman, which quoted him saying, "the purpose of the exhibit is to spark conversation and promote understanding and tolerance of diversity in society." During its campus run, a public discussion forum was held that featured a panel made up of university professor Sabrina Brinson, youth services public librarian Phyllis Davis, and community youth organizer Christine Peoples. During the forum, which was well attended, each of the panelists spoke on the importance of diverse literature to the growth and development of youth. Several MSU teacher education instructors gave assignments to their classes that centered on the exhibit's content.

In conjunction with the showing of the *Telling a People's Story* exhibit, AG Ford spoke at several venues in the city. Several of his book illustrations were featured in the exhibit. During Ford's talks he described his journey to becoming a professional book illustrator and gave drawing demonstrations. He followed each of his presentations with lively question-and-answer sessions with the audience. These and other celebratory events were planned by the Springfield AARI steering committee and implemented with assistance from volunteers and organizational employees (see Figure 3-1).

Meet New York Times Best-selling Illustrator

AG Ford

AG Ford, the illustrator of best-selling children's literature, will discuss his work, the process of making picture book art, and becoming an illustrator during two free Springfield events. All ages are welcome.

Thursday, March 28

- 2-3 p.m. in the Missouri State University Meyer Library auditorium 101. Books will be available for purchase and signing from 3-4 p.m. in Meyer Library Room 107. For information call 836-4547.

- 7 p.m. in the Library Center auditorium. Books will be available for purchase and signing after the event. For information call 882-0714.

Ford's work has appeared in over 30 books published for children, including "My Daddy, Dr. Martin Luther King Jr." and "Malcolm Little: The Boy Who Would Grow Up To Become Malcolm X," both featured titles in the traveling exhibit Telling A People's Story: African-American Children's Illustrated Literature.

Ford's visit is part of the 10th anniversary celebration of the Springfield African American Read-In, which funded his visit, with additional support from the Children's and Young Adult Book Review Board of Missouri and the Springfield Regional Arts Council.

Don't miss the traveling exhibit Telling a People's Story: African American Children's Illustrated Literature. You can see it at the Library Center, 4653 S. Campbell Ave., through March 31; and at the Duane G. Meyer Library, Missouri State University, April 3-May 22.

The exhibit Telling A People's Story: African-American Children's Illustrated Literature is organized by the Miami University Art Museum through a grant from the Martha Holden Jennings Foundation.

FIGURE 3-1. Publicity Flyer for AG Ford for Library Center Speaker Event, March 28, 2019.

Courtesy of Springfield-Greene County Library District.

School librarians and academic librarians often collaborate to build programs that prepare students at the middle and high school levels for college readiness or full-time careers post high school. Strengthening the former partnerships was a goal of a America Library Association (ALA) interdivisional committee between the Association of College & Research Libraries (ACRL) and the American Association of School Librarians (AASL), of which I was a member. The interdivisional committee created a toolkit that is posted on the ACRL website. One of the items in the toolkit is a Collaboration Checklist (Figure 3-2). The checklist provides steps for building partnerships and recommends networking to develop strategies to help academic librarians and school librarians to work better together.

Rationale
Academic and school librarians serve as liaisons to their respective institutions. They perform parallel functions at their sites: collection management and instruction to support curriculum. They also theoretically serve all their parallel respective constituencies: students, faculty, administrators, and selected community members (e.g., parents, alumni, local agencies, etc.).
Steps:

- Identify counterpart librarian
  - feeder schools/school for graduates
  - library staff contact information

- Make initial contact
  - schedule meeting
  - find common ground
  - share informal needs and successes

- Librarians gather data about their respective institutions
  - library mission, resources, facilities, staffing, instruction (including documents), library usage
  - clientele demographics, information literacy competency, curriculum, typical library-related assignments
  - analysis of data if possible, such as information literacy gaps
  - means to address information literacy gaps

- Set up follow-up contact meeting
  - share data
  - share information literacy instruction/learning activities
  - determine juncture of information literacy competencies

FIGURE 3-2. ACRL/AASL Interdivisional Committee on Information Literacy Toolkit, Collaboration Checklist

Maintained by ACRL Student Learning and Informational Literacy Committee 2016. Originally created by AASL/ACRL Interdivisional Committee on Information Literacy. Reprinted with permission.

- ○ design method of informing respective faculty of issues (e.g., speak to each other's faculty about information literacy needs and gaps; include IHE students who can talk to their high schools about information literacy needs)
- (optional) Set up regional librarians meeting
  - ○ each librarian identifies and contacts peers
  - ○ arrange meeting time/place/PR/supplies
  - ○ agenda: discuss efforts to this point by original librarian pair, set up way to communicate and coordinate efforts regionally
- Librarians work with their respective faculty
  - ○ share information literacy standards and issues with respective faculty through staff development/meetings
  - ○ identify curriculum
  - ○ design instruction
  - ○ implement instruction and assess process and results
- Set up follow-up contact (F2F or online)
  - ○ share efforts and results
  - ○ bring a faculty member (and student) to the meeting to share experiences and broaden support base
  - ○ discuss how to involve more faculty and articulate information literacy instruction
  - ○ develop a database or repository structure to gather information literacy instructional documents (e.g., assignments, presentations, assessments)
- Follow up faculty meeting between sites
  - ○ share information literacy efforts by subject domain
  - ○ articulate information literacy standards, instruction, and assignments
- Librarians and teachers work with their respective site personnel
  - ○ develop a school-wide information literacy initiative: standards, learning outcomes, scope, and sequence
  - ○ develop a repository of learning activities and assessments
- Hold regional summit about information literacy
  - ○ assess student learning (improvement, hopefully)
  - ○ train others in use of repository/database

FIGURE 3-2. *Continued*

The checklist provides suggested steps on how librarians from secondary schools and academic librarians can form networks and build strategies for developing student information literacy. I suggest that the same collaborative steps can be used for development of programs that promote African American writers and their work and other diverse literature. Such programs will teach students cultural literacy and respect for differences. This process could be part of cooperation across schools within a district for development of intentional collection development in school libraries and intentional library cultural programming in schools.

The mission of the Springfield AARI is to promote African American writers and build a community of lifelong learners and readers. The local mission aligns with the literacy initiative of the National African American Read-In leadership organization. Our local group follows the National Council of Teachers of English (NCTE) principles that champion building writing and critical thinking skills, along with reading, as exemplified in the NCTE organizational motto that encourages persons to "Read/Write/Think" (http://read.write.think.org).

Library programmers can design programs to promote student writing in conjunction with promoting exemplary African American writers. These programs that combine reading and writing curricula to promote African American and other diverse writers of young adult literature in K–12 schools offer opportunities for school librarians to form partnerships with language arts classroom teachers. This pedagogy aligns with the National School Library Standards. Featuring African American writers in these programs who serve as role models will provide a bridge for next-generation writers.

In the inaugural event of the Springfield AARI, a writer's workshop was held for a diverse group of middle school and high school students titled "Finding Your Voice." The workshop was taught by the late, legendary children's and young adult author Patricia McKissack. Similar workshops can be held by groups that borrow the latter model. Every writer's workshop need not be taught by a premier author. Classroom teachers, librarians, or even college graduate students might serve in that capacity. The important element of any writing workshop for youth is to provide exceptional reading materials. Providing reading and writing examples for youth that they can relate to and where they can see themselves portrayed positively will inspire them to read and write for enjoyment as well as for learning.

BUILDING PARTNERSHIPS BASED ON COMMON GOALS

The Springfield AARI strengthens its literacy programming by building relationships with SPS and other community stakeholders involved in literacy projects. The goals of the Springfield AARI to promote African American writers and to help build a community of readers are accomplished, in part, by developing partnerships with others in the community that have common or similar goals as ours.

For example, Springfield AARI developed relations with the organizers of a group named Children's Literature Festival of the Ozarks, which is partly composed of retired and active K–12 teachers. The latter organization hosts an annual festival for children that includes book talks and book signings by children's book authors. The festival has been held for more than thirty-five years. The Children's Literature Festival of the Ozarks organizers, in partnership with the AARI, worked together to arrange extended visits of some of the African American children's book authors who participated in the festival. These authors' extended stays provided an outreach to an AARI audience base of children and their families.

The Springfield-Greene County Library District is a public library system and a partner of the Springfield AARI. In another example of coordinated efforts, the Library District assists in developing and writing grants in support of library programming for the group. The AARI was awarded a grant to sponsor two workshops, one for children and another for educators. These workshops were facilitated by award-winning children's book illustrator and author Shane Evans.

The Springfield-Greene County Library District librarians hold book talks to read books by African American authors during children's reading hours. African American culture–themed books are not only read during Black History Month but year-round. Some of the librarians have experience serving on the national Coretta Scott King Book (CSK) Award Committee and other literary children's book award committees. They planned a mock jury discussion of children's books by African American authors related to the CSK Award as part of the AARI tenth anniversary celebration, which coincided with the fiftieth anniversary of the CSK Award.

Annually, the Springfield AARI participates in a Multicultural Festival held in Springfield during the month of January on the Martin Luther King Jr. holiday. The festival is organized by Unite of Southwest Missouri, Inc., a nonprofit community newspaper and online information service. The festival is a public event and features booths of different kinds and programming to celebrate various cultures and civic and economic development in the city and region. Participants enjoy browsing the booths and taking part in activities. The Springfield AARI, in partnership with the Ozarks Literacy Council, provides free children's and young adult books with cultural diversity themes to visitors of our booth. Some of the books are written by African American authors.

In striving to fulfill the goals of the Springfield AARI, we have built community partnerships that help to broaden our reach. I recommend to readers that they take a partnership approach with organizations with which they have common goals to expand outreach efforts and strengthen community engagement.

PARTNERSHIPS THAT PROMOTE AFRICAN AMERICAN POETS AND WRITERS

Developing programming around African American poetry is a mainstay of mine. African American poetry has broad appeal that attracts many persons, from those who enjoy engaging as audience members listening to poetry readings to those who enjoy participating as reciters of poetry to those who enjoy both listening to and reading the written word of poetry.

Poetry readings are an inexpensive library programming service to offer. These programs can be produced with modest cost, especially if space is available within your library or freely available within your organization to hold the event. If you do not have enough space, find cosponsors who will agree to provide desirable space to accommodate a reading. Besides space and volunteer poetry readers, hosting a poetry program may only involve providing light refreshments for the audience on the day or evening of the program. See the case example provided here of an African American poetry reading held during a National Poetry Month celebration, in April, at Salisbury University.

NATIONAL POETRY MONTH READ-IN: AFRICAN AMERICAN POETRY

By Stephen Ford

At Salisbury University (SU), located in Salisbury on Maryland's rural Eastern Shore, members of the SU Libraries' Diversity and Inclusion Committee partnered with faculty from the Education and English departments to create a read-in event celebrating African American poetry during National Poetry Month in April 2019.

Faculty librarians Stephen Ford and Angeline Prichard teamed up with Drs. Shanetia Clark (Education), April Logan (English), and John Nieves (English). Nieves is our resident poet expert. We planned to hold the event in the Dr. Ernie Bond Curriculum Resource Center, a library facility within the education school's building. To prepare for the event, the librarian members of the team identified library-owned books of African American poetry within our collections, solicited suggestions from our expert team members, and purchased additional books that we did not own. Students, faculty, staff, and the local community were invited, through various public relations venues, to attend and read works from their favorite African American poets. We arranged the space for the event with seating and a podium and included two microphones—one on the speaker's podium and one in the back of the room, which we hoped would embolden students and others to read aloud, especially those who were less used to the spotlight. To smooth the way, we provided light refreshments as well. The team invited the City of Salisbury's inaugural, and newly named, poet laureate, Ms. Nancy Mitchell, to serve as our main orator. She agreed, which turned out to be the first event of her laureateship. Dr. Shanetia Clark agreed to serve as our moderator during the evening.

On the night of the event, with a backdrop of original artwork by Eastern Shore native and award-winning African American illustrator/author Bryan Collier, we turned the lights down low to create a more relaxed atmosphere. We showcased the broad array of books of poetry on a portable display in the front of the room where we also provided copies of an African American poetry bibliography and the lyrics of Kendrick Lamar's album *Damn*, which won the 2018 Pulitzer Prize for Music.

The thirty people attending the read-in included a mix of faculty and their children, students, and several local community members. Poet laureate Mitchell was dynamic, truly knowledgeable about African American poetry, and an amazing reader. So were the other faculty and community members in attendance, reading with a full range of emotion, power, and conviction. Dr. Clark facilitated with a light touch, encouraging a free-flowing, natural participation. One remarkable reading stood out: a recording that Dr. Clark played of her father, who is a preacher with a deep and commanding voice, reading two Langston Hughes poems. The recording sparked a rousing and appreciative applause from our audience. With encouragement from their professors, all students in attendance read works aloud, usually from the glow of their smartphones. We listened to a mixture of known and less familiar poetical pieces, ranging from those in print collections to music lyrics.

The read-in was a triumph! After its conclusion, many hung around with a sense of giddiness, which we took as an excellent sign of success. Our desire is to transform the event into a larger, more prominent annual SU campus event to celebrate the diversity and inclusiveness of our campus, our community, and our culture.

Stephen Ford is the coordinator at the Dr. Ernie Bond Curriculum Resource Center, Salisbury University, Salisbury, Maryland.

The Springfield AARI and other groups or organizations that I've worked with have organized poetry writing workshops, poetry readings, and poetry competitions for youth. The Springfield AARI has held large-scale, variety, educational–cultural programs that incorporated some poetry readings, and entire programs based on a single poetry reading performance.

Poetry reading events can be planned, particularly for teenagers or young adults, in an "open mic" style or design. Another poetry program design that is popular among youth are slam competitions. Slam poet and assistant professor Javon Johnson provides a definition of "slam" in his book on the topic.

> The poetry slam is the competitive art of performance poetry. It puts a dual emphasis on writing and performance, encouraging poets to focus on what they are saying and how they are saying it. In contrast, spoken word can happen in an open mic format without structured competition or scoring. Traditionally, poetry slams consist of multiple poets who are judged by five randomly selected audience members. Immediately following each performance, the judges rate the competitor, using a rubric with a low of 0 and a high of 10, encouraging decimal points in order to decrease the chance of ties. The bout manager drops the highest and lowest scores and averages the middle three scores, and the total may range from 0 to 30. The rules of individual venues vary. . . . (2–3)

Slam competitions may contain profanity or sexually explicit content. It's wise to organize them with guidelines and rules of conduct. Slams are often popular among college students and older adult audiences as social gatherings and literary events. University student organizations and other youth organizations are possible cosponsors who may agree to partner with libraries to offer slams.

Often, library programmers can find poetry program partners on college campuses and within communities at-large among persons who are involved in poetry troupes or repertory theatre. The latter was the case in both Bloomington and Springfield in my programming experience. At Indiana University (IU), I collaborated with students from a theatre repertory group called Black Curtain, as well as with other students. The library at the IU Neal-Marshall Black Culture Center collaborated with these students by providing a welcoming space for students interested in organizing a semi-regular event during the evenings. After hours at the library, students held an open mic freestyle poetry event.

At Missouri State University in Springfield, an undergraduate student named Taylor Vinson founded a poetry troupe named Untamed Tongues. The Springfield AARI recruited Vinson and other members of the troupe to read their original poetry at several read-in programs. In addition, the troupe's founder was invited by the Springfield AARI to facilitate a poetry writing workshop for high school students that was very successful.

Library programmers may collaborate with schools and civic organizations to help develop local youth poetry performance and writing talents. Two such programs are the Poetry Out Loud and the ACT-SO competitions. Poetry Out Loud is a national arts education program sponsored by the National Endowment for the Arts and the Poetry Foundation that began in 2005. In cooperation with local schools and arts agencies, Poetry Out Loud prepares students to develop poetry interests and to compete in local high school, state, and national-level poetry performance competitions.

Since 1978, the NAACP has sponsored a local and national achievement program and competition for high school students known as ACT-SO (the Afro-Academic, Cultural, Technological and Scientific Olympics). Students can display their poetry talents in this competition.

Literary programs in libraries can promote established African American poets and writers by featuring them in special guest presentations. It's advantageous to have partners to assist in covering these speakers' expenses. Furthermore, cosponsorship may help to broaden audience participation. A case example is provided here that describes several literary endeavors that showcase writers of color. The programs are sponsored in partnership with faculty and staff at North Carolina Central University in Durham.

DEVELOPING LIBRARY PROGRAMMING THAT UPLIFTS AUTHORS OF COLOR

By Jamillah Scott-Branch and Vernice Riddick Faison

For the past twelve years, the James E. Shepard Memorial Library at North Carolina Central University (NCCU) has committed time and resources to develop author-centered events. For instance, the library's Marketing Committee was established. The committee's charge or objective is to intentionally and enthusiastically acknowledge, collect, and elevate publications by authors of color. The planning process for this endeavor incorporated the scholarship of our faculty and the input of our staff, students, and the greater community at-large. To showcase authors of color, the library has established the Faculty/Staff Publication Showcase and the James E. Shepard Memorial Library Authors' Club. These entities were developed to enlighten and educate our campus and community at-large about scholarship produced and to connect researchers, authors, and librarians for cross-collaboration. Furthermore, the library curated a collection of faculty/staff publications that are prominently displayed and made accessible for research and borrowing.

Faculty and Staff Publications Showcase

Music recordings, peer-reviewed research articles, monographs, art, conference posters, and book chapters are among the numerous submissions that have been received for our Faculty/Staff Publications Showcase. The showcase planning process involved selecting a visible area within the library where a large exhibition could be arranged to display scholarships of all forms. The Marketing Committee determined that the outreach effort for this event would involve librarians' communications to faculty in their assigned departments to encourage faculty members to share their scholarly materials. Likewise, the invitation could be extended to staff. Faculty and staff were required to register for the showcase and to provide library staff with a print copy of their current research to be displayed. Participants were afforded the opportunity to discuss their work. The library prepared a discussion area that included a podium with a microphone and a seating area for attendees. Another microphone was provided for attendees to ask questions of the authors. The library required that the publications submitted were published within the past three years. Over four hundred publications have been showcased as a part of this library programming series.

James E. Shepard Memorial Library Authors' Club

The Marketing Committee established the James E. Shepard Memorial Library Authors' Club in the fall of 2014. The club features authors who are affiliated with NCCU, as well as local and national authors who address NCCU community issues and interests. Librarians and support staff identify, solicit, and showcase authors with books that address an array of topics and were published within the requirements for date of publication. Since its establishment, the club has featured a multitude of authors covering topics ranging from African American experience in Durham, North Carolina, to the first integrated college basketball game between NCCU and Duke University under the veil of the Jim Crow South. The club became so popular that it attracted authors from surrounding communities, who contacted the library eager to be featured as a part of its series.

The Authors' Club and the Faculty/Staff Publications Showcase have been supported and well received. They are embraced by faculty, students, staff, and the NCCU community. Collaborations have been fostered between the library with faculty from different academic disciplines. Through informal conversations and from direct feedback, the library was informed that our events are valued and appreciated because they offered a platform for authors not only to showcase their work but to discover and learn from other authors. Additionally, faculty collaborated with the library staff to incorporate class time for students to attend the library-hosted book discussions. Faculty have rewarded students with extra credit for attending library book discussions when their scheduled class time did not conflict with the book discussion time. Instructors have required students to submit assignments based on works featured in the showcases.

Upon presenting at the Faculty/Staff Publication Showcase and book discussion, the guest author becomes an official member of the James E. Shepard Memorial Library Authors' Club and is awarded a personalized gift. Attendance at the book discussions is free and open to students, faculty, staff, alumni, and the public. Ten authors have been inducted into the club since its inception in 2014.

NCCU takes pride in its Faculty/Staff Publications Showcase and the James E. Shepard Memorial Library Authors' Club. These programs support lifelong learning and engage, educate, and entertain our faithful patrons. More importantly, they bring new people into the library and allow it to uplift the voices of authors of color.

Jamillah Scott-Branch is the assistant director of Library Services at James S. Shepard Memorial Library, North Carolina Central University, Durham, North Carolina.

Vernice Riddick Faison is head music librarian at James S. Shepard Memorial Library, North Carolina Central University, Durham, North Carolina.

As campus library head of the IU Neal-Marshall Black Culture Center Library, I hosted a program that came to be known as the Library Evening Extravaganza. It was billed as an informal dinner gathering followed by all types of board games and card playing. The sensational dinner menu featured bar-b-que ribs, macaroni and cheese, baked beans, greens, cornbread, and cake! However, the dinner event was a means to attract hundreds of students of all races and backgrounds; the true highlight of the evening were African American faculty authors who would each give brief talks about their most recently published books while seated at an honorary table during the dinner. During the informal gathering, after the dinner, African American faculty authors would stay to mingle with the students, giving them a chance to ask questions about the books and research that they had learned about earlier in the evening and to get to know African American faculty members on an informal basis. On a campus of about thirty thousand FTE students, with only a few African American faculty members, it was rare for many of the students to have a class taught by an African American faculty member or any faculty member of color. Students looked forward to the annual Library Evening Extravaganza as an entertaining program, and faculty looked forward to sharing their books among students who they hoped to teach in one of their classrooms. Figure 3-3 shows the program of the tenth anniversary of the Library Evening Extravaganza,

FIGURE 3-3. Program NMBCC Library Evening Extravaganza 10th Anniversary Celebration and Reception

which contains the names of faculty members who presented throughout the years.

Over the course of my career as an academic library programmer, I've always considered persons from the universities and communities-at-large who have joined with me in the work of producing programs as partners. Many students that I've worked with at both the university and high school level have accepted mentored leadership roles in the library programs that I've coordinated, becoming partners. Youth have participated as preprogram planners, emcees, and performers. I enjoy sharing the joy of African American literature and writings with youth; I am inspired by their creativity. Furthermore, youth bring their friends and peers, parents and other relatives to join as supportive audience members to programs.

Members of the Springfield AARI steering committee Nora England, Charlotte Hardin, Gwendolyn Marshall, and Rosalyn Thomas served as mentors to the youth who were involved in the programs that the read-in group sponsored. These and other committee members have strong ties to community and long histories of working closely with local youth populations, in schools, churches, and other organizations. The aforenamed and others worked closely over the years with the Springfield AARI and helped to build beneficial partnerships with teachers, librarians, and other civic organizations throughout the community. Springfield AARI committee members help to produce the educational cultural programs that grow our literacy initiative and make it thrive.

SUMMARY AND BENEFITS OF PROMOTING AFRICAN AMERICAN WRITERS

This chapter lays the groundwork to conceptually consider forming programming partnerships to promote African American writers and African American literature and other diverse literature. Included in the chapter are my four "Keys to Successful Collaboration," a content section titled "Pointers for Developing K-16 Partnerships," and the "Collaborative Checklist" borrowed from the former ACRL/AASL Interdivisional Committee for Information Literacy. Additionally in the chapter are found seven case examples by four contributors from different institutions, who share their implementation of reading and teaching and learning programs through partnerships to promote African American writers. I also share in the chapter more than half a dozen examples from my career of building programming partnerships to promote the reading of works by African American writers. More than a dozen case examples are found in this chapter.

The examples show how libraries' involvement builds bonds in community and helps community development. Partnerships are good for development in multiple areas: 1) building relationships that strengthen a library's ties to the community, 2) decreasing burdens on any one organization by spreading the workload and costs among different groups, 3) demonstrating unique strengths of libraries and other organizations, and 4) spawning new ideas for collaboration across organizations.

In conclusion, I'll comment briefly about why diverse writers and literature are important to the growth and development of youth and to future society.

Early literacy is a foundation building block for later success from elementary education to college education, the K–16 pipeline. Children who develop an appreciation of literacy even before and during preschool years are receiving a major building block for the development of their educational scaffolding (Darling-Hammond, 2010, 33–34). Exposing African American children at an early age to books written by African American authors increases their self-esteem and confidence, encourages their reading, and increases their reading levels, which can help to close educational attainment gaps. According to research, having diverse books in schools leads to "prejudice reduction" among all young readers because more positive, realistic, and multidimensional images are shown of all ethnic and racial groups (Banks, 1993).

Promoting and reading outstanding works written by African American writers affirms African American culture and heritage to readers. All persons benefit from accurate portrayals of different races and cultures, as expressed well in the essay "Mirrors, Windows, and Sliding Glass Doors" by the educator Rudine Sims Bishop (1990).

Library program planners are utilizing libraries for the public good by promoting cultural–educational programs, such as the ones discussed in this book to promote the works of African American writers. Evidence shows that library programs advantage all segments of communities by helping to develop culturally competent citizens and by fostering intercultural communication and understanding (Robertson, 2005, 1–7).

To round off this chapter, the following chart lists "Potential Partners for Promoting African American Writers," which includes broad categories. I have worked with many of these categorical partners throughout my career. If you extend an invitation to partner with these groups, I'm sure you'll meet many persons who will welcome the opportunity to form partnerships with you.

After-School Programs (all types)
Black Churches
Black Greek (Panhellenic) Organizations
Black Social and Civic Clubs
Community Civic Centers
K–12 Schools (private, public, and home schools)
Libraries of All Types (school, public, academic, and special)
Local Large Businesses (banks, etc.)

Local Small Businesses (barbershops and beauty salons, etc.)
Parents, Grandparents, & Other Caregivers
Universities and Colleges (diversity divisions, academic departments, student affairs units)

In Chapter 4, the reader will find many more program ideas. In Chapters 5 and 6, I will look back to look forward. I will share some of the assessment tools that I've used, as well as other techniques, to evaluate programs. Furthermore, I'll cover how assessment information from the former can be disseminated to your partners, supervisors, and other community stakeholders to help garner continued programming support. Lastly, I'll discuss how reflectivity and intentionality make programs stronger. I'll delve into the definitions of the two terms: what they mean philosophically and they mean practically.

REFERENCES

AASL/ACRL Interdivisional Committee on Information Literacy. "Collaboration Checklist." In ACRL AASL Toolkit on website maintained by the ACRL Student Learning & Information Literacy Committee, http://acrl.libguides.com/slicl/aasl. Accessed December 8, 2019.

Banks, James A. "Multicultural Education: Historical Development, Dimensions, and Practice." In *Review of Research in Education*. Edited by L. D. Hammond. Washington, DC: American Educational Research Association, 1993, 3–49.

Bishop, Rudine Sims. "Mirrors, Windows, and Sliding Glass Doors." *Perspectives: Choosing and Using Books for the Classroom* 6, no. 3 (Summer 1990): ix–xi.

Darling-Hammond, Linda. *The Flat World and Education: How America's Commitment to Equity Will Determine Our Future*. New York: Teachers College Press, 2010.

Harper, Afton. "Traveling Exhibit Promotes African American Culture through Children's Book Illustrations." *The Standard* (April 16, 2019): 10.

Johnson, Javon. *Killing Poetry: Blackness and the Making of Slam and Spoken Word Communities*. New Brunswick, NJ: Rutgers University Press, 2017.

National Council of Teachers of English. "Read/Write/Think." http://read.write.think.org. Accessed June 21, 2022.

Robertson, Deborah A. "Making the Case for Cultural Programming." In *Cultural Programming for Libraries: Linking Libraries, Communities, and Culture*. Chicago: ALA Editions of the America Library Association, 2005, 1–7.

4

Identifying African American
Writers for Programs

OVERVIEW

This chapter contains tips for identifying African American writers for programs that are fun and informative and that meet the needs of schools, universities, and wider communities. It provides guideposts to find African American writers for the purposes of promoting reading, diversity, and literacy, while at the same time giving directions to build partnerships around these shared program goals. I include examples from my experience in finding African American writers, which I featured in programs while serving as head of the Indiana University (IU) Neal-Marshall Black Culture Center (NMBCC) Library and while coordinating programs with the Springfield African American Read-In (AARI) in Missouri.

The chapter features case examples written by librarians and others located in different parts of the country who hosted programs around African American authors and utilized partnerships. The cases are from both before and during the COVID-19 pandemic period of 2020–2021. A case example from before the pandemic is written by Sophia Sotilleo of Lincoln University in Pennsylvania, and another is by Shanika Heyward of Indianapolis Public Library in Indiana. Case examples of programs held during the pandemic period are provided by librarians Jamillah Scott-Branch and Vernice Riddick Faison of North Carolina Central University and from staff persons of the Prince George's County Memorial Library System (PGCMLS) in Maryland. Chief Executive Officer Roberta Phillips and Chief Organization Officer for Communication and Outreach Nicholas A. Brown of PGCMLS write about their library system's strategic plan implementation, in which the sponsorship of programs featuring African American writers and other diverse writers is an integral part.

All the programmers who share their ideas have taken positive approaches to library programming and working with people while demonstrating strong leadership. The latter characteristics, in addition to having a passion for programming, are elements that fuel successful programs! Regarding the topic of this book, this means believing in the importance of reading and the contributions of writers, particularly African American writers. Enthusiasm breeds enthusiasm! During my thirty years of experience in promoting African American writers in library programs, at times I took the lead in proposing programs and at other times my partners took the lead in suggesting collaboration project ideas for consideration.

There are many African American writers to choose from when planning library programming. How does one make choices about which ones to build a program around? Who are the African American writers most likely to attract an audience and draw new users into your library? This book is designed to help readers find answers to those and other questions.

In this chapter, case examples describe partnerships formed with special collections and archives at universities that led to identifying African American writers to promote. If you don't live in a community with a university or public library that has a special collection, you can seek out a partnership with a local historical society or the state library, which may have source information about African American writers who were born in the state, lived in a local geographical area, or who write about local regional topics. These institutions may have materials that can be borrowed free of charge to create programs.

Secondly, African American writers who have received literary awards or other major recognitions are excellent choices that may attract large audiences and to build programs around. This chapter has a list of helpful websites to search for current, exceptional African American writers who have received awards or special recognitions. Literature scholars, colleague librarians, or other programmers can recommend writers to be featured in book clubs or in programs. One may choose to bring these authors to one's city or town to deliver presentations.

Lastly, this chapter discusses finding new or little-known local African American writers and other diverse writers who are "hidden gems." Librarians and other programmers can help these local talents to get readership by providing a forum for them through programs. In this way, programmers help expand the number of writers of color in the public sphere by nurturing them and giving them a healthy start to becoming known among a circle of readers and possibly to get published, if they are unpublished.

IDENTIFYING AFRICAN AMERICAN WRITERS THROUGH SPECIAL COLLECTIONS AND ARCHIVES

While I served as head of the library in the newly built NMBCC at IU, the library, in partnership with the special collections and archives of Lilly Library at IU, celebrated the centennial of the publication of W. E. B.

Du Bois's *The Souls of Black Folk*. The celebration included a special exhibit highlighting the book and its author and a book lecture presented by the IU chairperson of the African American and African Diaspora Studies Department, Dr. Valerie Grim. This was among the first of several collaborations between the NMBCC and Lilly during my years at IU.

W. E. B. Du Bois (February 23, 1868–August 27, 1963) was a sociologist, historian, civil rights activist, and author. He was the first African American to earn a PhD from Harvard University. Among Du Bois's many writings is the classic book *The Souls of Black Folk*, which was published in 1903 (Du Bois, 1903). Those of us at IU were likely among the thousands worldwide celebrating the hundredth anniversary of the publication of the book, a collection of essays and poetry about race in America. It is a seminal work in African American literature that contains the oft-quoted lines written by Du Bois about African American identity, which has been referred to as "double-consciousness." These lines describe the African American identity pulling in two directions—one side that yearns for a denied African homeland because of slavery and the other side that describes the pain of the constant struggle for the freedom and full citizenship promised by the ideals of American Democracy. Du Bois writes,

> One ever feels his twoness,—an American, a Negro; two souls, two thoughts, two unreconciled strivings; two warring ideals in one dark body, whose strength alone keeps it from being torn asunder.

The commemoration exhibit for *The Souls of Black Folk* was created in the NMBCC Library's state-of-the-art, floor-to-ceiling, inset exhibit case that faces the entrance of the library that visitors see when they enter. African artifacts, on loan from Lilly librarian Elizabeth Johnson and from the collection of William Itter, adorned the background of the exhibit case. The exhibit foreground featured a first-edition copy of *The Souls of Black Folk* and other works by Du Bois. In addition, the exhibit held original archival copies of signed letters between Du Bois and another American author and social activist, Upton Sinclair.

A collaborative, public service partnership grew between the NMBCC Library and the Lilly Library. On one occasion, Lilly Library loaned materials to the NMBCC Library to place on exhibit in conjunction with an exhibit at the Lilly Library. The exhibit provided outreach to a wider, more diverse audience than if it had been shown at just one of the libraries. The exhibit shared between the Lilly Library and the NMBCC Library was of books from the Limited Editions Club Collection featuring five oversized monographs of works written by Black writers and/or illustrated by renowned African American artists. Curator of Books at Lilly Library Joel Silver delivered a talk about the monographs. The Limited Editions Club Collection was started in 1929 by George Macy. The books were commissioned as finely rendered editions of classic works for distribution to a limited number of subscribers. In its entirety, the volumes published by the club beautifully showcase the work of many accomplished writers, printers, and modern artists. Figure 4-1 shows the program for the Limited Editions Club Book Exhibit at the two libraries.

In another example of a collaboration with Lilly Library, involving the promotion of Afro-Caribbean music lyrists, Lilly Library assisted in the setup of a traveling exhibition of post-WWII movie posters and calypso music memorabilia, which was on loan to the NMBCC Library from the Historical Museum of Southern Florida. "The Calypso Music in Postwar America Traveling Exhibit" was displayed in the NMBCC Library and an adjacent area. Calypso music is a type of native folk music that originated in Trinidad and Tobago and spread to other parts of the Caribbean. Lyrics are often a form of bantering that is part of entertaining competitions seen and heard during carnivals. The music became popular outside of the Caribbean after WWII and was even showcased in American movies. The exhibit included movie posters and album covers such as those featuring actor/singer Harry Belafonte. Another poster in the exhibit featured well-known poet Maya Angelou, who earlier in her life spent some time as a calypso singer.

The opening reception for the exhibit, which included Caribbean-themed food and a calypso and reggae dance band, was attended by hundreds. A two-day symposium on the indigenous origins of calypso music was held with lecturer Ray Funk, a collector of calypso-related items and an expert on calypso music and the carnivals that surround it. The widely viewed exhibit was held at the NMBCC Library for a semester.

The calypso music in the post-WWII exhibit drew scholarly as well as general-interest audiences. IU held several special collections related to the exhibit, including the internationally recognized folklore collection, the Archives of Traditional Music; African American Popular Music and Culture Archives/Center; and Black Film Center/Archive. The exhibit project was collaboratively sponsored and funded by the NMBCC Library, the African American and African Diaspora Studies Department, the Latin American and Caribbean Studies Department, and the Folklore and Ethnomusicology Department, all with the support of an IU Multicultural Initiative Grant.

Librarian Sophia Sotilleo contributes to *Promoting African American Writers* with another illustration of working with special collections and archives at a university to find African American writers. Sotilleo provides a case example about retrieving "forgotten" archival materials by African American writers for students to discover anew for research projects. Several curricular plans are described, including one in which Sotilleo, in collaboration with several professors in the English Department and the Visual Arts Department, develops a pilot learning experience for a class by using books from the library's Broadside Press Collection.

African American Cultural Center Library
Neal-Marshall Black Culture Center
275 N. Jordan Avenue

Mon-Thu 9:00am-9:00pm
Fri 9:00am-5:00pm

Lilly Library
1200 E. Seventh Street

Mon-Fri 9:00am-6:00pm
Sat 9:00am-1:00pm

Book Exhibit

The Limited Editions Club

INDIANA UNIVERSITY
LIBRARIES
B L O O M I N G T O N

Five monographs, illustrated by renowned
African American artists

Exhibited February 2004 at the
Indiana University Lilly Library, Lincoln room
and displayed individually in turn at the
African American Cultural Center Library
January- June 2004

African American Cultural Center Library
Exhibit Schedule, January - June

January-February

The First Book of Moses, Called
Genesis: the King James Version 1989
Bible. Old Testament. Genesis
Silkscreens by Jacob Lawrence

March

For my People 1992, c1989
Margaret Walker
Lithographs by Elizabeth Catlett

April

Sunrise is Coming After While 1998
Langston Hughes
Silkscreens by Phoebe Beasley

May

Music, Deep Rivers in my Soul 2003
Maya Angelou
Color etchings by Dean Mitchell

June

Poems of Léopold Sédar Senghor 1996
Léopold Sédar Senghor
Silkscreen prints by Lois Mailou Jones

The Limited Editions Club Collection was started in 1929. The private enterprise of Mr. George Macy, the books were commissioned as finely rendered editions of classic works for distribution to a limited number of subscribers. Each volume bore illustrations by highly regarded contemporary artists.

The Club was first carried on by Macy's own family and has endured to the present in hands as faithful to its qualities. In its entirety, the volumes published by the Club beautifully showcase the work of many accomplished writers, printers and modern artists. The Lilly Library and African American Cultural Center Library are pleased to present five African American works from among those Club editions, which Indiana University is fortunate in having acquired.

Please join us for a:

Book Talk

Tuesday, February 3, 2004
"For Readers and Collectors - 75 Years of The
Limited Editions Club"- Joel Silver,
IU Lilly Library Curator of Books
12:00- 1:00 p.m.

**Indiana University
Neal Marshall Black Culture Center
Elizabeth Bridgwaters Lounge, Room A115**

Book Talk and light luncheon sponsored by
The Office of Multicultural Affairs, Lilly Library,
and The African American Cultural Center
Library

FIGURE 4-1. Book Exhibit Program, the Limited Editions Club, Five Monographs Illustrated by Renowned African American Artists

Dudley Randall (January 14, 1914–August 15, 2000), a poet, librarian, and World War II veteran, founded the Broadside Press in Detroit, Michigan. Randall ran this small press during the 1960s and 1970s, when there was a surge of Black literary artists arising from what became known as the Black Arts Movement. Due to racism, many of the poets during that period initially found it impossible to overcome racial barriers and get published in the White-dominated, mainstream publishing industry. Many of these poets found a home in the Broadside Press.

At Lincoln University, Sotilleo uncovered a treasure trove of Broadside Press poets from the archives at the Langston Hughes Memorial Library. Some of the names of poets whose works were present included Nikki Giovanni, Sonia Sanchez, Yusef Iman, Sam Greenlee, Amiri Baraka, Askia Muhammad, and Philip M. Royster. Students were inspired by the poets whose works they read from books in the Broadside Press Collection. They wrote poems of their own, which they then self-published.

Furthermore, Sotilleo arranged a trip for the students to attend a poetry reading given by one of the poets, Patricia Smith, whom they were introduced to from the Broadside Press Collection. Students met with the poet after the reading and had an opportunity to speak with her and to ask her questions about her life and poetry.

"ACCESS TO TREASURES"

By Sophia Sotilleo
Division of Academic Affairs
Lincoln University, Pennsylvania

The Langston Hughes Memorial Library at Lincoln University houses treasures in the form of books, periodicals, and archived materials. As the first Afro-Latina librarian to serve as the access services librarian, I was amazed at how much information we have written by Black writers as well as about Black people. We also have collections that speak to monumental times in the history of People of Color as well as the rich history of Lincoln University. Information on movements like the Pan-Africana Movement, Civil Rights, Renaissance, and so much more are housed in the library, only being used by certain research scholars. Realizing the treasures hidden in this building, I was on a mission to plan programs that would encourage collaboration and allow access to our Black writers' collections. This is where my passion for programming and collaboration began. The programming and collaboration projects started with the English Department under the Pan-Africana track.

First, we placed the Broadside Press Collection on course reserve for the creative writing course. This collection contains published works by important writers from Gwendolyn Brooks to Haki Madhubuti, Alice Walker, Etheridge Knight, Audre Lorde, Amiri Baraka, Nikki Giovanni, and Sonia Sanchez that were barely being used. Particularly, for a class with a focus on Black poets that includes an assignment for students to create their own poetry around any social justice theme, I knew reading these pieces would spark some creative ideas for the students. I then created an information literacy session specific to doing research on the authors and on their specific topics. This included various types of resources from several types of databases and finding aids. To keep the excitement of the class going, we received approval to take students to hear and meet one of the poets being researched—Patricia Smith. The outing reinvigorated the class and took the students to the final stretch of the course to create and publish their final pieces.

At the end of the semester, each student created their own publication of poetry that included artistic work for the cover of their books. Including artistic pieces to the project was a bonus. It allowed the library and the English Department an opportunity to collaborate with the Visual Arts Department. This project ended with the library hosting a book reading. Students' final projects were displayed, and the students read selected poetry from their books. Everyone was invited to hear each student author read from their poetry book. The audience was filled with faculty, staff, family, and friends. We then catalogued the books and added them to our Lincolnian collection, which features published Lincoln authors. This project increased the circulation of our archived collection of poetry written by Black writers from the Lincolnian collection, as well as through interlibrary loan requests. The course was offered for two academic years with the library program embedded in the coursework.

The next project on which I collaborated was the senior seminar course focused on African American literature. I was so delighted to learn that the professor was looking forward to working with me again. This journey took us to a capstone project that resulted in a twenty-five-page paper (single spaced), a ten-minute presentation of the final paper, and an electronic portfolio of the writing process and the students' academic career. I began by creating a Libguide that featured African American literature in different time periods. After the Libguide was completed, an information literacy session was developed that focused on scholarly research to assist with finding information for the literature review.

I created a makerspace in the library for the senior seminar class. This dedicated space allowed students to read all the books that they found on their topics. They found it exciting to know that there was a dedicated space just for them to sit and read. Their classroom professor and I were proud to see the students reading and enjoying the space that was created. Students stated that they enjoyed the dedicated time for reading. It established a routine that was necessary to ensure success for the course.

In the end, the programming and collaboration for both courses were a great success. This partnership established an ongoing relationship between the English Department and the library that promotes access to Black writers. It also started numerous opportunities with other departments that I look forward to working with.

Sophia Sotilleo is associate professor/access services librarian at Langston Hughes Memorial Library, Lincoln University, Pennsylvania.

When librarians and other programmers uncover little-known special collections and archives within universities, state libraries, and public libraries, they should highlight what they find to raise public awareness about exceptional and sometime rare materials. Academic libraries and other libraries may have resources available such as technological support to provide special programs like what is described at Lincoln University in Pennsylvania. Unique exhibits and programs may be created using these newly found materials, through collaborations, to enhance a library's outreach.

Use of exhibits can be a simple way to attract community interest by shining a light on forgotten African American authors. What if your library or organization doesn't have access to a large exhibit space? Library programmers can develop exhibits by using existing space and repurposing the space to create attractive physical displays of books using existing shelving or other areas of the library. Exhibits that promote African American writers can be made on digital platforms with images of book covers or other items in an established virtual space. The displays can be a showcase to raise public awareness about an African American writer or a group of African American writers based on a theme or a genre.

For example, the Springfield AARI developed an exhibit using a basic display case at one of the city's branch public libraries as part of a Black History Month commemoration. The exhibit focused on the poetry of five African American women writers and contained biographical facts about the poets. The Black History Month exhibit included books of poems by Maya Angelou, Gwendolyn Brooks, Rita Dove, Tracy K. Smith, and Alice

Walker. The five poets represented three generations. Three of the five were recipients of Pulitzer Prizes for poetry. Brooks was the first African American writer in the United States to be awarded the Pulitzer Prize, which she received in 1949 for her book of poetry *Annie Allen*. Dove won the Pulitzer for her verse-novel *Thomas and Beulah* (1986). Smith was an awardee of the Pulitzer for poetry for her 2011 collection of poems, *Life on Mars*.

FINDING HIGH-INTEREST AFRICAN AMERICAN WRITERS LEADS TO GREAT PROGRAMMING

The Basic Idea of Matching Programs to Community Interests

In considering which African American writers to promote, think of the assets of your library or organization, as well as the needs and wants of the communities that you serve. There are African American writers or themes in writing that your communities will likely welcome and enjoy. Find a match between your library's resources, your community's wants and needs, and themes when developing library programming.

Library programmers from all types of libraries and programmers in other organizations should consider great African American writers from different historical periods to recognize and to promote in programming. Choose writers from the Harlem Renaissance such as novelists Langston Hughes or Nella Larsen, or from the late twentieth century and early twenty-first century like rappers and lyricists Tupac Shakur and 2018 Pulitzer Prize for music winner and rapper Kendrick Lamar. Choose African American writers like Zora Neale Hurston, whose contributions were forgotten and then rediscovered in the 1970s by African American writer Alice Walker. Hurston had been ignored in the study of American writing and in the canons of American literature and anthropology. Programs provide public recognition of African American writers who may, like Hurston, be at risk of being forgotten. Programming helps to keep African American writers' names alive among new generations of readers and moves their names from the margins to the forefront of education and cultural learning.

In 2014, five important African American artists who helped shape the twentieth century died: Maya Angelou (April 14, 1928–May 28, 2014); Amiri Baraka (October 17, 1934–January 9, 2014); Ruby Dee (October 27, 1922–January 11, 2014); J. California Cooper (November 10, 1931–September 20, 2014); and Walter Dean Meyers (August 12, 1937–July 1, 2014). The Springfield AARI presented a program in February 2015 titled "Tribute to the African American Pen" to commemorate the passing of these great authors during 2014. During the program, participants read aloud poetry or excerpts from the writings of each of these extraordinary writers.

Nobel Prize laureate Toni Morrison died on August 5, 2019. Morrison, the first African American writer to win the Nobel Prize in literature, was born Chloe Anthony Wofford on February 18, 1931, in Lorain, Ohio. She left to the world a great writing legacy and a torch for other writers to carry forward. Her writing concentrates on African American history and culture in all its pains, triumphs, and joys. Library programming can help to carry forward her literary gift for coming generations to enjoy. In June 2019, a documentary film was released that chronicles her life titled *Toni Morrison: The Pieces I Am*. The film can be an interesting backdrop for a discussion program on Toni Morrison, her life, and her literary work (Morrison, 2019).

SAUL WILLIAMS AT INDIANA UNIVERSITY (IU) IN THE 2000s

In the year 2000, Saul Williams (February 29, 1972–), then a new rising star who would become a trailblazer slam poet, arrived in Bloomington, Indiana, as a guest of the IU Black Culture Center Library. The library was being housed in a residence hall while the Neal-Marshall Black Culture Center (NMBCC) and Theatre Department complex was under construction. At that time, Saul Williams, although a performer who had captivated audiences in his lead role in the 1998 independent film *Slam*, was relatively unknown and was not the star that he was to become. He had not yet performed in the 2013 Broadway musical *Holler If Ya Hear Me*, featuring Tupac Shakur's music, or in his other movie acting roles. He had published his first two books of poetry, *The Seventh Octave: The Early Wrings of Saul Stacey Williams* and the *She* (with a square root sign over the "he" in the one-word title), but he hadn't yet published his several other books of poetry and albums of music that were to follow.

I found Williams's name in a catalog of speakers that I borrowed from the university's student activities office. I happened on the small listing and short biography of Williams, who had an exceptionally low speaker's fee attached. I was able to afford to bring him to IU as a guest speaker with the small programming budget I had as the head librarian for the Black Culture Center Library. I don't recall approaching the student activities office or anyone to be a cosponsoring partner. I contacted Williams's agent and completed a contract basically on my own. I publicized the Saul Williams two-day speaking engagement as hosted exclusively by the Black Culture Center Library. It was a free event that was open to the entire IU student body and university community.

The agreement with Williams involved him leading a student poetry writing workshop and giving a poetry reading at Woodburn Hall. He led the workshop for about forty student writers in the temporary space of a university residence hall utilized during the construction of the new Black Culture Center. Williams also gave a poetry performance to a "packed to overflow capacity" audience of about three hundred persons in the auditorium-style lecture classroom of Woodburn Hall, where he allowed two students to present their original poetry as an opening act to his hour-plus-long poetry presentation performance. It was a sensational yet surreal experience for all attendees. The crowd, which appeared to be mainly undergraduate students, was very racially diverse, and Williams mesmerized all with his theatrical performance of hip-hop and a variety of poetry genres.

Williams was to make at least one comeback visit to perform at IU; one was sponsored in part by the IU Student Activities Office. He presented at IU's Whittenberger Auditorium, in the student union building, which at the time was one of the largest student union buildings in the United States. Williams continued to tour U.S. universities and other venues worldwide to perform his poetry. His slam and hip-hop-inspired poetry were featured in an exhibit at the National African American Museum of History and Culture in Washington, D.C., in 2019.

Williams's first IU visit in 2000, hosted by the Black Culture Center Library, as successful as it was, represents some of the challenges I faced as an African American librarian at predominantly White universities. The audience response to Williams's poetry presentation was a surprise to me, in part, because I had received very little administrative support or feedback regarding the publicity that I had formally distributed throughout the campus. His presentation was an instance in which I did not seek out partnerships for funding because I had a budget from the Office of Multicultural Affairs to cover it. In planning a campus visit by Williams, I decided to save time and to negotiate only through the Office of Multicultural Affairs. I did not feel at ease in navigating through library administrative channels because of past bad experiences that I perceived to be racist.

At colleges and universities, open dialog is needed between administrators (possibly deans at the library, student affairs, and academic department level) and library staff, along with other community stakeholders, about partnerships for library diversity programming for successful and well-organized programs. Studies are needed to address how best academic libraries, as cultural institutions in the United States, can demonstrate more commitment to diversity programming and outreach. What resource investments, in time and money, are needed institutionally to support library diversity programming and to support the librarians who develop, coordinate, and lead in these programming efforts?

STAYING CURRENT ON EXCEPTIONAL AFRICAN AMERICAN WRITERS

Where does one go to find exceptional new and contemporary published title lists by African American writers? There are library and publishers' journals that publish book reviews, but reading these often requires that readers pour through many pages of reviews to determine books with African American characters or nonfiction profile personages or an explicit reference to books that are written by African American authors. Some library professional and industry journals with book review content are *BookList, Choice, School Library Journal, Library Journal, Kirkus,* and *Publishers Weekly.* Some magazines and scholarly journals that review books and specialize in reviewing works by African American and African diaspora writers are the *Black Book Review* (https://qbrbookreview.com), *Black Scholar,* and *Essence.*

Another source to find African American writers' publications is book award announcements. One can look to the Coretta Scott King (CSK) Book Awards to discover African American authors of meritorious children's and young adult literature as well as outstanding African American book illustrators. The CSK Awards, founded in 1969, have been awarded annually for more than fifty years. A listing of winners of the CSK Award is kept on the award sponsor's website, the Ethnic & Multicultural Information Exchange Roundtable (EMIERT) of the American Library Association.

The Black Caucus of the American Library Association (BCALA) Literary Awards have actively recognized outstanding writing of African American authors for more than twenty-five years, since 1994. The BCALA Awards honor books in the areas of fiction, nonfiction, first novel, poetry, and in "Outstanding Contribution to Publishing." Each year, since 2015, the BCALA has recognized the best self-published e-books in the categories of fiction and poetry. The BCALA Literary Award winners are announced annually on the BCALA website.

The NAACP Image Awards celebrated its fiftieth anniversary in 2019. The awards are given in several literary categories, including biography/autobiography, children, debut author, fiction, instructional, nonfiction, poetry, and youth/teens. These awards are announced annually.

Popular and scholarly reading websites and social media offer recommendations of African American–authored books and other diverse literature, such as the websites weneeddiversebooks.org and WellReadBlackGirls.org. Library programmers can conduct research using reputable websites and social media to find listing of writings by African American writers, as well as inspirational programming ideas for the promotion of African American writers. Websites include the following:

- http://aalbc.com (African American Literature Book Club "Celebrating our literacy legacy since 1998—Black Literature is for Everyone")
- http://bcbooksandauthors.com (Black Children's Books and Authors)
- http://ccbc.education.wisc.edu/booklists/ (Multicultural resources from the Cooperative Children's Book Center at the University of Wisconsin)
- http://diversityinya.tumblr.com (Young adult diversity book lists and literacy tips on Tumblr)
- https://ncte.org/get-involved/african-american-read-in/ (National Council of Teachers of English, African American Read-In)

- http://thebrownbookbookshelf.com (African American and other diverse literature)
- www.weneeddiversebooks.org (Nonprofit organization with tips on finding and using diverse books)
- http://rif.org (Nonprofit organization Reading is Fundamental provides activities and multicultural book lists)
- http://www.wellreadblackgirl.org (Started in 2015 by sisters Shayna and Shayla Vincent as an Instagram page, the site expanded to include a nationwide book club for girls ages 7–17 and sponsors a Brooklyn literary festival)

GO LOCAL TO FIND TALENTED AFRICAN AMERICAN WRITERS

African American writers may be right in front of you but overlooked. To find local, burgeoning African American writers in your city, state, or region, explore talent within local K–12 schools, colleges and universities, and community writers' groups. African American writers may be found through library outreach programs by asking attendees to sign up if they are interested in sharing their talent. With a little exploration, librarians and others can discover "hidden" talent, such as self-published or small press authors within local African American communities. In her case example following, Indianapolis public librarian Shanika Heyward describes her successful sponsorship of an annual showcase of local African American authors from within her library's community.

AN INDY PUBLIC LIBRARIAN'S CALL FOR AUTHORS

By Shanika Heyward
Regional Manager
Indianapolis Public Library

The Indianapolis Public Library, East Thirty-Eighth Street Branch, in Indianapolis, Indiana, is in one of Indy's high-crime and poverty-stricken areas; however, people come from all around the city to attend our book clubs, Author Spotlights, and Annual African American Author Fair. My most successful partnerships are with local African American authors. My mission is to give every author a VOICE, and my vision is to develop a community of readers and lifelong learners.

For the past six years, I have provided both agent-published and self-published authors with a night to shine brightly by hosting an Author Spotlight. Authors are given an opportunity to discuss their book(s), meet new potential readerships, and be applauded for their accomplishments. The library purchases copies of the authors' books to add to our library's system, and each book receives a "local author" sticker to ensure readers know they're reading a book from a local author. Many of the local authors have developed faithful followers and book clubs using their books as a map to unlimited success. Some authors have established their own consulting businesses to help people fulfill their full potential or improve their quality of life.

Other authors have used the feedback from Author Spotlight to develop multiple books. One of the most successful local African American authors that I've featured here is a young woman named Shay Spivey. She wrote her first nonfiction book, called *How to Submit a Winning Scholarship Application*, and the library used it to develop a Scholarship Workshop Series. The series' target audience was struggling families in my service area with young people who have a desire to attend college but can't due to financial hardship. The scholarship workshops were held as a means of highlighting Shay's first book and several other books written by her that were very successful: *Find Free Money for Graduate School*; *How to Find Scholarships and Free Financial Aid for Private High School*; *Free Tuition College for Adults 50+*; *Prepare for College Senior Year Checklist*; *Free Tuition Colleges*; *Prepare for College in Middle School Checklist*; *Socks for the Homeless: A Community Service Project*; *Prepare for College*; *Educate Girls around the World*; and *Where to Find Free Money for College*.

The Eastside Tutors Inc. is a local tutoring agency in the area that tutors struggling readers and learners. The group founder and owner, Tonia Sanders, partnered with the library to support a writing project in which the children in her group cowrote a book called *The Eastside Authors: A Collection of Children's Stories*. These struggling readers and learners *rewrote* their own story, one for success and unlimited opportunity, because they understand that readers are leaders and leaders are readers.

My most recent mentoring success, and the biggest of all, is a former library employee who started working in the library as a teenager. We developed a mentor-mentee relationship. His name is Brian Robinson, and he wrote two books, one for girls and one for boys, titled: *The MI Own Collection: For Him: Volume 1: Therapeutically Traveling through Time* and *The MI Own Collection: For Her, Volume 1: Therapeutically Traveling through Time*. Brian takes readers on a voyage to places where pitfalls transform into healing and happiness into hope.

Every first Saturday in June, authors are invited to serve on an author panel or to be an author at an author table during the East

38th Street Annual African American Author Fair. This fair engages readers and gives them the opportunity to meet local writers and other reading enthusiasts.

Let's celebrate the love of reading with our African American brothers and sisters!

Shanika Heyward is regional manager at Indianapolis Public Library.

Next is a case example of a highly successful partnership between a university library and academic departments and other university units. It describes partnerships that were developed by the James E. Shepard Memorial Library at North Carolina Central University with the university's Office of Faculty Professional Development and the unit of Information Technology Services to host a virtual program with an alumni writer during the COVID-19 pandemic of 2020–2021.

PANDEMIC PARTNERSHIP PROGRAMMING

By Jamillah Scott-Branch and Vernice Riddick Faison
North Carolina Central University

The COVID-19 pandemic forced our library to rethink how to engage users in cocurricular programming activities strategically. James E. Shepard Memorial Library (Shepard Library) at North Carolina Central University (NCCU), like many libraries worldwide during the pandemic, had to adjust, adapt, and alter the way we provide many of our services and resources to our students and faculty. The Shepard Library, which serves as our main library for undergraduate and graduate research, remained open during the pandemic for students, faculty, and staff who wanted to utilize our services. The library's marketing committee was tasked with devising an engagement plan to keep communication lines open with our campus community and to help with the use of a plethora of digital tools available at the library or freely available on the internet. Library staff wanted to continue to support authors and host events deemed important to faculty and students. To accomplish this, the committee partnered with campus stakeholders such as the Office of Faculty Professional Development (OFPD) and Information Technology Services (ITS).

At the start of the pandemic, and for the entire summer of 2020, Shepard Library's administrators held weekly staff meetings that included updates from the director of Library Services, departmental updates, staff wellness checks, and discussions to determine how to proceed with library services and programming. The marketing committee decided unanimously to identify and intentionally partner with other campus entities. The overarching goal of establishing or, in some cases, reestablishing, collaborative partnerships was to ensure that library staff did not duplicate efforts. The library's marketing committee decided to host our signature Authors Club event designed to promote recently published authors. We partnered with campus stakeholders to design and promote a full roster of new virtual events to interact with and engage our campus community.

When the pandemic began in the United States, Shepard Library stopped all individual and group in-person information literacy classes and sessions and switched entirely to all-virtual information literacy sessions. Cisco WebEx is the official video conferencing application used on the campus of North Carolina Central University. The administration wanted the librarians to be comfortable providing virtual instruction and hosting a virtual workshop; therefore, they arranged for personnel from the Department of Information Technology services to conduct a WebEx workshop for the library staff.

James E. Shepard Memorial Library Authors' Club (Virtual Book Discussion)

In the fall of 2014, the James E. Shepard Memorial Library's marketing committee established the James E. Shepard Memorial Library's Authors Club. The club has sponsored and featured authors who are affiliated with North Carolina Central University and local and national authors who address NCCU community issues. Each academic year we feature authors whom we have sought out and authors who have sought us out to express their desire to be featured in the Authors Club. An array of topics has been covered and discussed. A family medical doctor explained how to avoid the superwoman complex. A professor of history explained how soccer is a major sport in Latin America, and another professor of history discussed the African American experience in Durham, North Carolina. A former historian at the Smithsonian Institution and a *New York Times* best-selling author discussed the first integrated college basketball game between NCCU and Duke University under the veil of the Jim Crow South, and more.

Due to the COVID-19 pandemic, Shepard Library suspended all in-person programs and events. The library's marketing committee felt that it was essential to explore programs and events that we could successfully conduct virtually to continue to engage our users. Though we had never facilitated any online or virtual events, we concluded that perhaps a book talk would be the best event for us to sponsor for the first virtual event. In August 2020, a 1976 alumnus, Barbara L. Peacock, emailed the assistant director of Library Services at the library to inform her that she had released her third book and sent a complimentary copy to the library. The assistant director received the book, informed the alumna of the Authors Club, and inquired if she was open to sharing her book with the club. The assistant director shared this information with the director of Library Services and the marketing committee. They subsequently extended Dr. Barbara L. Peacock an invitation to become the first feature author with our newly created Shepard Library virtual Authors Club book Talk Series. The title of the featured book was *Soul Care in African American Practice*.

The marketing committee members were excited about hosting the book talk in this new venue, but we also had a slight uneasiness. We designed and created a promotional event flyer to be shared on all social media accounts and emailed it to students, faculty, and staff for more prominent promotion and exposure. After consulting ITS (Information Technology Services) regarding our options, we decided that Cisco WebEx would be the best solution for hosting our virtual book talk. This technology solution provided library staff the ability to create an event that allowed for greater control of who entered the virtual program and who was muted or allowed to speak. It has a panelist feature that allows the marketing committee event facilitators and featured speakers to be panelists with the ability to speak during the book talk. It also allows for greater event control because audience members cannot unmute or interrupt the event. Once the event was created and the panelists established, a unique link was generated and emailed to all the panelists that enabled them to attend the actual event. It also generated a different link for attendees of the event. The attendees' link was inserted in the flyer, and the flyers were advertised, posted, emailed, and distributed throughout the NCCU community and afar.

Because this was our first virtual event, we met with Dr. Peacock prior to the event to go over the logistics, familiarize her with WebEx, and address any questions that she might have. The Authors Club featured Dr. Peacock and her book *Soul Care in African American Practice* in a virtual program held on November 11, 2020. The marketing committee facilitated the event, including a welcome, a brief history of the Authors Club, acknowledgment of some previous topics discussed, and an introduction of the featured author. Dr. Peacock's book talk included a short PowerPoint presentation that addressed African Americans allotting time out of their regular schedules to care for their soul through spiritual practices. This was a very informative book talk, and Dr. Peacock really engaged the attendees. The book discussion was followed by a question-and-answer session. After the discussion was officially ended, we still had attendees who stayed on the video conference. They did not leave until we literally exited the WebEx session. Our first virtual event was a huge success. Once we gained knowledge in hosting virtual events, more virtual events were forthcoming.

Jamillah Scott-Branch is the assistant director of Library Services at James S. Shepard Memorial Library, North Carolina Central University, Durham, North Carolina.

Vernice Riddick Faison is head music librarian at James S. Shepard Memorial Library, North Carolina Central University, Durham, North Carolina.

The Prince George's County Memorial Library System (PGCMLS) in Maryland incorporates all three elements that I posed early in the book that must come together for the benefit of best practices in excellent programming. These elements are the exceptional placing of "programming featuring African American authors," "promotion," and "partnerships" for the benefit of community audience learning and enjoyment. PGCMLS demonstrates programming best practices in the implementation of its strategic plan at the height of the COVID-19 pandemic and other social challenges.

PROMOTING BLACK AUTHORS & STORIES: LIBRARY PARTNERSHIPS ADVANCING CULTURAL AWARENESS

By Roberta Phillips and Nicholas A. Brown

During 2020, the United States was faced with three devastating crises: a global health pandemic, a flash point in the national reckoning with the murders of Black people by police, and an economic crisis exacerbated by systemic inequities that have existed for over four hundred years on these lands. The Prince George's County Memorial Library System (PGCMLS) in Maryland, which serves a majority-Black (64.5 percent) and Hispanic/Latin (19.5 percent) population (U.S. Census Bureau, 2021), had to move quickly to address the global moment authentically and substantively to demonstrate that public libraries have a role and responsibility to bring communities together. The combination of programs, information access, and social services that public libraries offer and support can be integral in creating a better future for Black Americans and other victims of injustice.

Beyond Prince George's County's current demographic makeup is a complex and painful history that highlights the injustices directed at Indigenous and Black people, as well as a local spirit of activism that saw early challenges to slavery in the courts by enslaved Prince Georgians in the late eighteenth century and early nineteenth century (Thomas, 2020b). Prince George's County is located on the traditional lands of the following Indigenous people—Mattapanient, the Patuxent, the Piscataway, the Moyaone, the Pamunkey, and the Accokeek, past and present. Additionally, the jurisdiction was the largest slave-holding county in Maryland in the nineteenth century (Maryland State Archives, 2019). Fast-forward to today, the urban, suburban, and rural 4444 disparities persist. PGCMLS's vision is to "provide a collaborative foundation within the community for all Prince Georgians to create the world they want to see" (PGCMLS Strategic Framework 2021–2024). In pandemic America in 2020, this translated into a public library system that connected customers with the stories, authors, and speakers who would give them the tools and inspiration to become active participants in the "good trouble" that it takes to stand up for race and social justice.

Highlighting the Black Experience

PGCMLS has a long tradition of providing thoughtful programming that encourages cross-cultural understanding and honors the lived experiences of those who have been oppressed locally and nationally, especially Black Americans. Like public libraries across the country, PGCMLS immediately ramped up its virtual programming and virtual customer engagement in the spring of 2020 to extend the community connections that customers love and appreciate from visiting their neighborhood branch libraries. Staff at every level of the organization recognized the importance of the library shining a direct light on the injustices taking place in our local and national communities daily. Programs accomplished this by inviting self-reflection, dialogue, and a deeper understanding of how the systemic injustices that Black Americans have been subjected to for more than four hundred years still exist in daily life, even in a very progressive and diverse community like Prince George's County.

The virtual library promoted essential services, provided access to information resources, and presented educational programs for all ages during the period when our buildings were not open to the public. As a customer-centered organization, PGCMLS's virtual programs focused on the topics interests of library cardholders shared via a customer survey conducted in spring 2020. There was a clear need for early literacy programs, creative outlets for youth to keep engaged with STEM and literacy, and programs for adults and seniors that would foster connections despite their quarantining at home for safety reasons. PGCMLS made a conscious decision early during the pandemic to dedicate many programming resources to conversations and programs that engaged customers in constructive dialogues about understanding race and social equity, with a focus on the Black experience in the United States. Programs were designed to cultivate empathy, which was measured through qualitative social impact stories rather than focusing on simplistic quantitative metrics like viewership data and program frequency.

During the pandemic, PGCMLS reaffirmed its commitment to celebrating the work of Black authors, poets, and creators, and the stories and journeys of Black Americans. The library has a responsibility to provide a platform for local and national authors to share their work and to provide customers with opportunities to hear directly from the leading thinkers of our time. In advancing programming focused on the Black experience, PGCMLS saw great value in collaborating with a range of local and national partners on developing and promoting programs. Curatorial and programming expertise were combined when the library launched a series called "The Elephant in the Room: A Diversity Dialogue," which is a monthly book-focused discussion program. These candid conversations between Michelle Hamiel, PGCMLS's chief organizational officer (COO) for public services, and Kyla Hanington, outreach coordinator, Prince George's County Office of Human Rights, became a beacon of light for members of our local and extended national community to gather and contemplate the work of authors like Dr. Ibram X. Kendi, Vernā Myers, Mahzarin R. Banaji, Steve L. Robbins, and Robin DiAngelo. These dialogues have been appreciated by many one-off and regular viewers who have shared comments like: "I am a fan! I follow all the Diversity Dialogues you hold" (September 20 email from a viewer in Tennessee). These diversity dialogues have succeeded in helping individuals learn from the range of experiences with racism that people face. Persons must evaluate their own biases and how they can better show up to combat racist acts.

PGCMLS's programming around race and social equity has included numerous speakers from diverse backgrounds, from Asian and LGBTQ+ to Hispanic/Latin and Muslim. In 2020, there was frequent emphasis on intersectional identity and the connections between the Black American experience and other identities. This approach was important to PGCMLS staff, as the points of intersection highlight the common adage that Black history is American history. Featured speakers like R. Eric Thomas (*Here for It*) and George M. Johnson (*All Boys Aren't Blue*) shared their experiences as Black queer men who live their whole and true selves (Johnson, 2020; Thomas, 2020a).

PGCMLS Goes Global: Dr. Ibram X. Kendi on *How to Be an Antiracist*

A turning point came when PGCMLS and its partners (Joe's Movement Emporium, Prince George's Community College's Center for Performing Arts, and Prince George's County Office of Human Rights) hosted Dr. Ibram X. Kendi for a discussion of his book *How to Be an Antiracist* in the weeks after George Floyd's tragic murder (Kendi, 2019). This event was copresented with nineteen public libraries in Maryland through Maryland State Library and exemplified how public libraries have the power to bring local, national, and global audiences together to learn about the issues of our time. Over 226,000 live viewers watched Dr. Kendi's talk, with another 100,000+ viewing on demand over a one-month period. The event prompted conversations about the pervasiveness of racism and unconscious bias throughout our local and global viewing community on social media and in living rooms. PGCMLS captures a Twitter post of a white family with young children sharing their dinner while watching the live broadcast. While the personal impact of the program is not necessarily measurable in this type of instance, the proactive posting of this moment by a customer on their Twitter account provided evidence of the content reaching multigenerational households who committed to hearing what Dr. Kendi had to say. On July 20, 2020, one patron posted:

> My thanks to @PGCLS for hosting a online great conversation with @DrIbram about how to be an antiracist. I was grateful for chance to learn, listen and reflect on my own straight, male, white privilege and how I can use it to be a better ally.

The success of the Dr. Kendi event led to the creation of Maryland Libraries Together, a programming collaboration among Maryland

Library Systems and the Maryland State Library, to host and promote author events statewide that address social justice and inclusion. Speakers featured in this series have included Isabel Wilkerson (presented by Howard County Library System), Devin Allen and DeRay McKesson (presented by the Enoch Pratt Free Library), a panel of public health and clinical professionals on the COVID-19 vaccine (presented by the Enoch Pratt Free Library), and a panel featuring a mix of leading Hispanic authors (Julia Alvarez, Angie Cruz, Reyna Grande, and Juan Felipe Herrera).

On the heels of the Kendi event, PGCMLS continued to expand its virtual speaker series to showcase authors whose work has had a transformative impact on our collective understanding of the Black experience. Programs featured Pulitzer Prize–winning author and columnist Leonard Pitts Jr. (a native of Prince George's County), former U.S. Poet Laureate and Pulitzer Prize winner Natasha Trethewey, Emmy-nominated actor Melvin Jackson Jr., Tricia Elam Walker, Anna Malaika Tubbs (*The Three Mothers*), National Book Award winner Andrew Aydin (coauthor, *March* series with Rep. John Lewis), and many more (Lewis et al, 2016; Tubbs, 2021). Over fifty virtual author/speaker events focused on the Black experience and race and social equity were presented between April 2020 and June 2021, along with numerous virtual read-alouds for young children, special programs for Juneteenth, and community conversations focused on local support services and resources. PGCMLS approaches cultural heritage programming as essential year-round. Limiting Black history and culture programs to just February each year, or LGBTQ+ programs to just Pride month in June, is incredibly limited in scope and does not adequately represent or serve the customers who would benefit from exposure to said cultural heritage education.

Hometown Authors

PGCMLS maintains a passion for celebrating and honoring authors who have ties to our local community. The library's very first virtual author event in April 2020 featured Dr. Renate Chancellor of the Catholic University of America (Washington, D.C.) in conversation about her book *E. J. Josey: Transformational Leader of the Modern Library Profession*. This event set the tone for PGCMLS's virtual programs, which are recognized for highlighting trailblazers whom we can all look to as role models for fighting for change (Chancellor, 2020). Throughout summer 2020, PGCMLS hosted a series of local author events that replaced an in-person local author expo that was impacted by the COVID-19 pandemic. The series featured authors like Aisha Rice, Austin Camacho, Shelly Ellis, and RJ Clayton, who are all passionate about providing tips of the trade to other local authors. The PGCMLS Foundation also presented a series of local author programs called "Antoine and Friends," hosted by children's author and local teacher Antoine Lunsford. Featured authors included Glen Mourning, Ebony Troncoso, Toni Settles, Christine Turner Jackson, Ciara Hill, and Melinda Rapp.

A lively discussion with Jason Reynolds, national ambassador for young people's literature, author of *Look Both Ways: A Tale Told in Ten Blocks*, and coauthor of *Stamped: Racism, Antiracism, and You*, was held in September 2020 (Reynolds, 2019, 2020). Reynolds grew up in Prince George's County, and his experience coming of age here informs much of his work. Clint Smith, a former Prince George's County high school English teacher and author of *How the Word Was Passed*, chose PGCMLS to launch the national tour for his book about the legacy of slavery in the United States. It was a thrill to have over thirty-five hundred live views for the launch and to partner with Loyalty Bookstores, a local independent bookstore owned and operated by a queer black woman, Hannah Oliver Depp. The library and bookstore partnership resulted in over sixteen hundred sales for publication day and helped the book rapidly reach the top of the *New York Times* nonfiction bestseller list.

Black Caucus of the American Library Association

Organizational partnerships are most effective when the parties involved have mission and values alignment and achieve greater impact when combining efforts. Following the tremendous reach of PGCMLS's July 2020 Dr. Ibram X. Kendi event, the library and the Black Caucus of the American Library Association (BCALA) came together to present the Black Voices series, which featured authors whose recent books consider contemporary life for Black people through a historical lens. Engaging the Black Caucus of the American Library Association was a natural next step as the organization was formed to serve as an advocate for the development, promotion, and improvement of library services and resources to the nation's Back diaspora. The partnership involved PGCMLS's programming team booking authors for the series and developing promotional materials, and then BCALA and PGCMLS combining efforts to promote the events nationally. This joint effort made important conversations available to a broad audience, while connecting viewers with the work

of both BCALA and PGCMLS as representatives of local public libraries across the country.

The PGCMLS and BCALA series, with events copresented by the
Prince George's County Office of Human Rights and Maryland Com-
mission on Civil Rights, featured appearances by Calvin Baker (*A
More Perfect Reunion: Race, Integration, and the Future of America*),
Dr. Michele Harper (*The Beauty in Breaking: A Memoir*), Bassey Ikpi
(*I'm Telling the Truth but I'm Lying*), and Eddie S. Glaude Jr. (*Begin
Again: James Baldwin's America and Its Urgent Lessons for Our
Own*) (Baker, 2020; Glaude, 2020; Harper, 2020; Ikpi, 2019). Bassey
Ikpi's *New York Times* best-selling *I'm Telling the Truth but I'm Lying*
is a collection of essays chronicling her journey with mental illness.
Ikpi's family immigrated to Prince George's County when she was
young, and PGCMLS had a formative role in providing her with a
space to learn and pick up books. She also wrote part of her mono-
graph in PGCMLS's Bowie Branch Library, a testament to the lifelong
impact public libraries have when they create welcoming environ-
ments where young people can see themselves represented on our
shelves and in our programs. These programs created a safe platform
for civic engagement and truth-seeking, covering contemporary issues
like the way healthcare disparities disproportionately affect Black
Americans and how historical perspectives on the Black experience
can still be guiding lights in dark times today.

Tackling the Issues

The library's ongoing collaboration with the Prince George's County
Office of Human Rights (PGCOHR) has led to dozens of important
programs with authors and civic leaders about topics like faith, disability awareness, and social justice. The series has featured authors
like Jennifer De Leon, Maria Hinojosa, and Michael W. Twitty and a
recurring series called "Voting: Democracy in Action." This series
evolved from initially combining historical commentary with practical
guidance on participating in the 2020 general election to exploring the
way history informs current civic issues. With support from Maryland
Humanities, the series extended through winter/spring 2021 to include
appearances by advocate Taos Wynn, Andrea Blackman of the City of
Nashville (former curator of the Civil Rights Room), Ed Morales, and
Azadeh Shahshahani. These events explored voter suppression, considering the 2020 Georgia Senate elections, the role of immigration in
elections, and understanding that Hispanics and Latinos are not a
monolithic voting bloc. PGCMLS's emphasis on Black history and

culture programming has strengthened staff's ability to curate cultural programs across disciplines and interest areas, a positive internal benefit that ultimately serves customers' interest in lifelong learning.

Conclusion: The Bigger Picture

The case study of PGCMLS collaborating with partners like BCALA to elevate the work and voices of Black writers and creators during the COVID-19 pandemic is just one example nationally of how public libraries can signal their commitment to racial and social equity for Black Americans. Programs can signal a library's values and priorities, especially when significant staff and financial resources are allocated to support specific initiatives—in this case, Black author and speaker programs. For a public library and its partners to truly effect systemic change on the local level, a strategy must be in place first and refined constantly. PGCMLS's work is rooted in its Strategic Framework, which highlights inclusion and literacy and learning as two of the library's focus areas. Programs are just one piece of the imperfect puzzle, along with communications, accessible and inclusive services, equitable recruitment and hiring practices, career development opportunities that overcome classism, and systems for adjudicating exclusionary incidents. PGCMLS is engaged in this introspective work, led by COO for Public Services Michelle Hamiel and a systemwide Race and Social Equity Team. While public library programs likely will not end or completely reduce racism in the United States, we do have the power to change hearts and minds one welcoming interaction at a time. Public libraries, through their programs and partnerships, can and should take a bold stance for human rights, starting with supporting Black customers by ensuring that Black voices and stories are a part of every opportunity for discovery and engagement.

Roberta Phillips is chief executive officer at Prince George's County Memorial Library System, Largo, Maryland.

Nicholas A. Brown is chief organizational officer for communication and outreach, Prince George's County Memorial Library System, Largo, Maryland.

SUMMARY

In this chapter, readers found programming ideas involving African American writers that were generated in collaboration with special collections and archives, such as those described between me, the librarian at the IU NMBCC Library, and the IU Lilly Library; and by Sophia Sotilleo of

Langston Hughes Memorial Library at Lincoln University in Pennsylvania and academic departments. In addition, a virtual program to promote African American alumni writers of North Carolina Central University and developed by librarians Jamillah Scott-Branch and Vernice Faison during the 2020–2021 COVID-19 pandemic was described. You may develop similar projects yourselves by building partnerships.

To assist you in finding published African American writers to feature in programs, in this chapter I listed websites of various library associations and nonprofit organizations to search for references to outstanding African American writers. I shared the story of Shanika Heyward, regional manager with Indianapolis Public Library, who describes coordinating literary programs that promote African American writers she's found by looking within her own community. She found and promoted burgeoning writing talent locally. She designed programs around these local writers who attracted audience members from around the city to join her library programs. Phillips and Brown provided a case study of exceptional value with ideas for virtual programming by showcasing events they sponsored with numerous partnerships during the pandemic period from 2020 through 2021.

In the next two chapters, I will look back to look forward. I will share some of the assessment reports that I developed, as well as techniques I've used to evaluate programs. Furthermore, I'll cover how assessment information like what I describe can be disseminated to your partners, supervisors, and other community stakeholders to help garner continued programming support. Lastly, I'll discuss how reflectivity and intentionality make programs stronger. I'll delve into the definitions of the two terms—what they mean philosophically and what they mean on a practical level.

REFERENCES

Baker, Calvin. *A More Perfect Reunion: Race, Integration, and the Future of America.* New York: Bold Type Books, 2020.

Brooks, Gwendolyn. *Annie Allen.* New York: Harper & Brothers, 1949.

Chancellor, Renate. *E. J. Josey: Transformational Leader of the Modern Library Profession.* Lanham, MD: Rowman and Littlefield, 2020.

County Health Rankings. *County Health Rankings & Roadmaps: Maryland.* University of Wisconsin Population Health Institute, 2021. https://www .countyhealthrankings.org/app/maryland/2021/measure/factors/65/data. Accessed June 5, 2022.

Dove, Rita. *Thomas and Beulah.* Pittsburgh, PA: Carnegie Mellon University Press, 1986.

Du Bois, W. E. B. *Souls of Black Folk.* Chicago: A. C. McClurg & Co., 1903.

Glaude, Eddie S., Jr. *Begin Again: James Baldwin's America and Its Urgent Lessons for Our Own.* New York: Crown, 2020.

Harper, Michele. *The Beauty in Breaking: A Memoir.* New York: Riverhead Books, 2020.

Ikpi, Bassey. *I'm Telling the Truth but I'm Lying: Essays*. New York: Harper Perennial, 2019.

Johnson, George M. *All Boys Aren't Blue: A Memoir-Manifesto*. New York: Farrar Straus, 2020.

Kendi, Ibram X. *How to Be an Antiracist*. New York: One World, 2019.

Lewis, John, Andrew Aydin, and Nate Powell. *March* (Trilogy). Marietta, GA: Top Shelf Productions, 2016.

Maryland State Archives. *Beneath the Underground: The Flight to Freedom and Communities in Antebellum Maryland*. Maryland State Archives, 2019. http:// slavery.msa.maryland.gov/html/antebellum/pg.html. Accessed June 5, 2022.

Morrison, Toni. *Toni Morrison: The Pieces I Am*. Timothy Greenfield-Sanders, Director, Magnolia Pictures, 2019.

Prince George's County Memorial Library System. "PGCMLS Black Voices Series Graphic." Prince George's County Memorial Library System, 2020a. https:// pgcmls.info. Accessed June 5, 2022.

Prince George's County Memorial Library System. "PGCMLS Eddie S. Glaude Jr. Graphic." Prince George's County Memorial Library System, 2020b. https:// pgcmls.info. Accessed June 5, 2022.

Prince George's County Memorial Library System. PGCMLS Strategic Framework 2021–2024. Prince George's County Memorial Library System, November, 2020c. https://pgcmls.libnet.info/strategic-plan/strategic-plan. Accessed June 5, 2022.

Reynolds, Jason. *Look Both Ways: A Tale Told in Ten Blocks*. New York: Atheneum Books, 2019.

Reynolds, Jason, and Ibram X. Kendi. *Stamped: Racism, Antiracism, and You*. New York: Little, Brown and Company, 2020.

Smith, Tracy K. *Life on Mars*. Minneapolis, MN: Graywolf Press, 2011.

Thomas, Eric R. *Here for It, or How to Save Your Soul in America: Essays*. New York: Ballantine Books, 2020a.

Thomas, William G. *A Question of Freedom: The Families Who Challenged Slavery from the Nation's Founding to the Civil War*. New Haven, CT: Yale University Press, 2020b.

Tubbs, Anna Malaika. *The Three Mothers: How the Mothers of Martin Luther King, Jr., Malcolm X, and James Baldwin Shaped a Nation*. New York: Flatiron Books, 2021.

U.S. Census Bureau. "Quick Facts: Prince George's County, Maryland." U.S. Census Bureau, 2021.

5

Library Programming Assessment and African American Writer Programs

WHAT IS LIBRARY PROGRAMMING ASSESSMENT?

Based on my reading about assessment over the years, I have settled on a generalized definition for library programming assessment. I view library programming assessment as an evaluation of impact or effect of a planned public event, a program, or a service on library users or potential new users. In the instance of library programs, library users can also be categorized as audience members. The literature about assessments states that either qualitative or quantitative methods can be used or a combination of these. In relation to the theme of this book, I will discuss both qualitative and quantitative methods of library programming assessment with a focus on diversity programs, particularly the evaluation of programs that promote African American writers. The programs being evaluated are ones that emphasize one or more of the following goal areas: 1) increasing library outreach, 2) building cultural competence, and 3) improving literacy development.

In addition, we may apply the mission or strategic goals of one's institution to the area of library programming and evaluate how well the mission is employed in carrying out programming. For example, is cultural diversity part of an institution's mission or one of its strategic goals? If yes, is there evidence of library programs that are designed and offered to promote cultural diversity?

Mary Catherine Coleman is a school librarian and was the 2017 recipient of the American Association of School Librarians (AASL) Collaborative School Library Award. In her book *Shared Foundations: Collaborate* (Coleman, 2020, 30–31), she discusses ideas on the development of school library mission and the assessment of collaboration projects that are aligned with the school's mission. In the area of cultural competence, she suggests two possible reflective questions for school librarians to ask themselves:

1. How might we witness cultural competency behavior in learners?
2. Who can I talk to in the building to help my understanding? (ibid., 37)

In this book, I provide suggestions of potential diversity program partners that library program planners can team up with (see Chapter 3). For example, K–12 school librarians and public librarians often work together around common goals. Why not team up to support African American writers? Academic librarians can and should also make it a priority to work with entities in the broader community and support reading works by diverse writers such as African Americans. Librarians or other program leaders can begin by having short conversations with friends, allies, and associates about programming ideas and efforts. The conversations can provide a sense of how programs are perceived. Some of the persons that one talks with may become "sounding boards" for ideas. Some conversational contacts may become partners who help to achieve diversity goals, such as promotion of African American authors.

Another source of assurance to library programmers that their intentional actions are making a positive difference is to examine how well their actions are matching up with the Core Values of Librarianship. These values were revised and adopted in a statement by the American Library Association (ALA) national council in 2019. The core values are what guide the professional practice of librarianship. Librarians can assess the development of their library programs and consider how well they reflect these values or principles. The core values are:

Access
Confidentiality/Privacy
Democracy
Diversity
Education and Lifelong Learning
Intellectual Freedom
Preservation
Professionalism
The Public Good
Service
Social Responsibility
Sustainability (Reprinted with permission. American Library Association, 2006)

In many ways, each of these professional values depends on the other like a web or fabric of many threads. Promotion of access to African American writers touches on many of these values. Providing information about and works by diverse authors contributes to community education and lifelong learning, democracy-building, diversity, the public good, intellectual freedom, preservation of history, and social responsibility.

African American writers are central to the telling of the true story and history of America as illustrated in such works as the novels of Pulitzer Prize–winning author Toni Morrison and the plays of Pulitzer Prize–winning playwright August Wilson. African American writers tell the American story with authentic voices and from unique vantage points.

Furthermore, an accurate and balanced portrayal of the American story is diverse and multi-perspectival. Programs to promote African American writers and other diverse writers are one way to share accurate representations and different cultural perspectives. Reflecting on how library programs fit with and support organizational and professional goals is a type of introspection and qualitative evaluation.

HOW TO DO ASSESSMENT OF PROGRAMS THAT PROMOTE AFRICAN AMERICAN AUTHORS

Following are lists of some quantitative and qualitative tools that may be used for assessing programs, including programs that promote African American writers.

Types of Quantitative Assessment of Library Programming

- Attendance counts
- Satisfaction surveys using Likert scales
- Demographic counts (age, race or ethnicity, education level, etc.)
- Comparisons over time of program attendance counts or demographic changes

Types of Qualitative Assessment for Library Programming

- Attendee feedback using on-the-spot interviews
- Partner and volunteer feedback (oral or written)
- Testimonial comments concerning programs from teachers, civic leaders, and others (thank-you notes, congratulatory letters, etc.)
- Focus groups
- Media coverage of programming (traditional and social media) to demonstrate a program's perceived public importance

LIBRARY PROGRAM ASSESSMENT EXAMPLES

Questionnaires are a tool that can be used to collect audience perceptions about programming. You can find within this chapter (Figure 5-1) an example of an evaluation form that is designed as a questionnaire that the

Program Evaluation Form

The Springfield African American Read-In Committee (AARIC) will continually strive to improve our programs. Your input into the program you recently attended will assist us with this process.

Program: Film screening of *Eyes on the Prize* (Episode 2)
Film Discussion Facilitator's Name: Dr. Gilbert Brown
Date: February 3, 2014

Please indicate your level of satisfaction with each of the following:

Program met my expectations	poor	fair	satisfactory	good	excellent
Program content	poor	fair	satisfactory	good	excellent
Ability of presenter to communicate content	poor	fair	satisfactory	good	excellent
Area in which program was held	poor	fair	satisfactory	good	excellent
Convenience of program day and time	poor	fair	satisfactory	good	excellent
Overall, how would you rate this program	poor	fair	satisfactory	good	excellent

If you answered "poor" or "fair" to any of the above, please indicate your reasons:

_____

_____

Would you recommend this program to friends or family?   Yes   No
How did you hear about this program?

_____

What changes, if any, would you recommend for this program?

_____

Do you have any suggestions for future programs?

_____

Additional comments:

_____

_____

Thanks for providing your feedback!

FIGURE 5-1. Program Evaluation Form, Program: Film Screening *Eyes on the Prize* Episode Two

Springfield African American Read-In (AARI) committee used to assess audience perceptions about a program it held at a university library, "Film Screening of *Eyes on the Prize* (Episode Two)." This program was a creative means of introducing the audience to the history of African American leaders from the twentieth-century Civil Rights Movement. The program was held as part of a commemoration for Black History Month. The evaluation form begins with a positive tone and a value statement from the members of the AARI committee saying we, "continually strive to improve our programs. . . . Your input into the program you recently attended will assist us with this process." The evaluation form is only one page in length, half of that being a few statements that program attendees can mark on a Likert scale about their level of satisfaction with the program. The other half of the questionnaire lists a few open-ended questions. The questionnaire asks a single yes/no question at its conclusion, but a very telling one, "Would you recommend this program to friends or family?" When a person is willing to recommend a program to a friend or family member, that's a very favorable endorsement!

A second example of a questionnaire comes from the evaluation of one of the earliest programs that was offered as part of the Springfield AARI literacy initiative. That program was a Young Writers' Workshop featuring author Patricia McKissack (Figure 5-2). The questionnaire asked demographic questions as well as open-ended opinion questions. Quantitative results (numerical counts) on the demographic

---

Evaluation—Young Writers' Workshop
Featuring Patricia McKissack—Oct. 17, 2009

Total Number of Participants = 40 approximately
Total Number of Evaluations = 26
Optional Information Given =
Males = 4
Females = 22
Teachers or Parents = 3
High School/Middle School = 14   5th & 6th Grade = 6   College Student = 1
Race: Black = 5   White = 15   White & Black = 1   Hispanic = 2
American Indian = 1   [24 persons]

1. **What is your impression about the time and length of the workshop? (feedback summarized)**

    Just Right = 18   **Too Long = 4**   **Too Short = 4**

    Sample comments:

    "It's nice time limit not too long and not too short, I think you got great information in that length of time."

    "It was good; I didn't even know time was passing."

    "I thought the time & length were good. I wish there was more time."

FIGURE 5-2. Survey Example, Evaluation Young Writers Workshop

"My impression is speaker's vigorous voice and she introduces her writing experiences."

"Just enough time, very good workshop, parents seem to enjoy it also."

"Good amount of time for the author to say everything she has to share, but perhaps a bit too long for the younger kids."

"Just right for kids; but I wish we were coming back for a part 2 afternoon."

"I've been touched! The two hours flew by!"

"Long—but worth it!"

"I think it was a pretty good length. Maybe more time to share our stories and ask questions."

"The time was just about right. Maybe 30 minutes more could be used for questions and comments."

"It was very good—I could have listened to Patricia McKissack for much longer!"

"It was very worth it."

"I think the amount of time plus the content of the workshop really made a difference."

2. **Tell us what you like best about the workshop. (summarizations)**

The stories that she read and storytelling = 18

Explanations of writing technique = 10

General ideas she shared = 9

Refreshments = 1

3. **Tell us what you liked the least about the workshop. (sample comments)**

"The time was longer than I thought"

"I think it would be all of us having to sit in the 3 front rows"

"Talking about fiction"

"I liked it all"

"Speaker introduces her three books"

"The cold temp of the room"

"One or two readings of her stories were good examples, but three was too many"

"I liked it all"

"Not enough interaction"

"I didn't like that the donuts were cold"

FIGURE 5-2. *Continued*

4. **Tell us what you would like to see improved about this workshop. (all comments)**

   "Let use read our stories"

   "More people need to come to these types of things"

   "I would like to see more people coming even through you can't help the outcome of who showed up it would be cool to see more people."

   "More time on non-fiction"

   "Maybe some talk about poetry"

   "More visual and physical activities"

   "More time and interaction one-on-one talking with the author"

   "I think there should have been more things we could have done to improve our writing skills, like the verb exercise."

   "More time to close would have been helpful to both the author and students"

   "Time to read poems"

   "The interaction time, more of it"

   "More people"

5. **If this workshop is offered in the future, I would . . .**

   Attend as long as I'm qualified   Yes = 26   No = none
   Recommend to my friends   Yes = 26   No = none

6. **What is your overall impression of the workshop? (all comments)**

   "Very fun"

   "I liked it a lot"

   "I loved it"

   "That it was wonderful and very exciting"

   "It was fun and very educational"

   "I liked it very much"

   "Speaker is beautiful voice to introduce her books"

   "I loved the workshop. I brought my two boys out to learn more about writing and reading. Something else besides sitting in front of the TV. I want my boys to continue to read and enjoy reading also. I was glad to offer my children something besides sports."

   "How much we learned from it"

   "I was very impressed. Ms. McKissack is a wonderful speaker with a lot of wisdom to share. Thank you for the opportunity."

   "I thought it was a wonderful workshop."

   "Inspiring!"

FIGURE 5-2. *Continued*

> "Terrific!"
>
> "I think that over all it was really good"
>
> "Good"
>
> "Very interesting and helpful for young writers"
>
> "It was very pleasant and I learned a lot"
>
> "I really enjoyed it, and it inspired me to write more."
>
> "This workshop gave me anew perspective on writing and how to make characters and settings fit."
>
> "It was very helpful"
>
> "Wonderful"
>
> "Very cool"
>
> "I loved it...broader look at African American authors [successful]"
>
> "I enjoyed it. I liked how Patricia shared things about her life, childhood, and herself."
>
> "...Very helpful; I learned a lot of things that could help me in my future writings."

FIGURE 5-2. *Continued*

composition of the audience, as well as a qualitative evaluation (a listing of answers to the open-ended questions), are shown here as provided by the respondents.

Yet another type of assessment might examine learning gains of participants in library programs. The Springfield AARI sponsors programs annually in February and other programs at irregular intervals, including workshops that provide opportunities for teaching and learning. One such program was a Poetry Workshop and Slam Competition for teens. We partnered with teachers from high schools and middle schools and parents to sponsor a two-hour Saturday morning Poetry Workshop and Slam Competition. Twenty participants attended the workshop. A college student senior, founder of a poetry troupe on her college campus and self-published author of a book of poetry, agreed to serve as facilitator. She received words of praise for her facilitation, a type of informal evaluation, from the teachers, parents, and youth who were engaged in the workshop.

The competition portion of the program was judged by a three-member panel of college teachers and staff. Participants in the workshop learned about poetry writing and performance techniques in an interactive teaching and learning format. First-, second-, and third-place contest winners received monetary awards and an opportunity to perform their poetry during two upcoming events. Winners were invited to perform their prize-winning poetry at the annual Springfield Chapter NAACP Martin Luther King Jr. Day Program and at the finale African American Read-In program held in February.

In this chapter is an example of a brief survey that was given to evaluate a panel program held on the topic of diversity in children's literature, which was held at a university library venue. The audience was made up mainly of teacher education college students and their instructors. The panel consisted of three presenters: a university professor, a community organizer, and a public library youth services librarian. A printed survey with a Likert scale was used in the program evaluation. In the survey, which was distributed to attendees immediately after the program, respondents indicate that they either strongly agree, agree, or are neutral, disagree, or strongly disagree with statements. Each response option is weighted (1–5) with 5 being the highest. The survey contained only four statements. Although there were forty student and other attendees at the program, only twenty respondents (50 percent) completed the survey. The results for each statement on the survey are shown in the chart below.

PANEL PRESENTATION EVALUATION

"Mirrors, Windows, and Sliding Glass Doors: African American Children's Literature"

Total Attendees at Panel = 40   Total Returned Surveys = 20

Circle the option that best represents your answer to the following (number of responses in parentheses):

1. The presentation met my expectations—Total Score 4.60
   Strongly Disagree (0), Disagree (0), Neutral (2), Agree (4), Strongly Agree (14)
2. I will be able to apply the knowledge learned—Total Score 4.95
   Strongly Disagree (0), Disagree (0), Neutral (0), Agree (1), Strongly Agree (19)
3. The panelists were knowledgeable—Total Score 4.90
   Strongly Disagree (0), Disagree (0), Neutral (1), Agree (0), Strongly Agree (19)
4. Adequate time was provided for questions—Total Score 4.75
   Strongly Disagree (0), Disagree (0), Neutral (1), Agree (3), Strongly Agree (16)

Another area of programming assessment might look at programming outreach efforts and examine numbers of potential new library users who attend a program. The Springfield AARI participates annually in the Springfield Multicultural Festival that is held during Martin Luther King, Jr. Day. The festival is a civic and cultural event sponsored by Unite of Southwest Missouri Inc. located in Springfield, Missouri. At the festival, the AARI Committee distributes information about our citywide literacy initiative. In addition, we give free multicultural-themed books to children and youth. We count the number of individuals who receive a book at the festival as a program contact. The festival is a means to promote our main educational and cultural AARI program that is held about a month after the date of the festival each year, usually during Black History Month. We have given away as many as 250 children's books each year. The festival is an opportunity to receive exposure and do outreach to a wide and diverse population. In 2020, more than two thousand persons attended the festival.

In some cases, tangible evidence of library outreach from patrons can be gathered during a program event or other type of program. During an event, on-the-spot reactions can be documented from social media or in traditional media interviews. In the case of library exhibits, guest books can be made available to collect names of visitors. A whiteboard can be made available near an exhibit area so that exhibit visitors can leave anonymous feedback or "sticky note" with comments about their perceptions. And if circulating books related to the exhibit theme are made available, then circulation numbers can be counted for the number of loans made on exhibit-related titles.

Another assessment tool that can be used to evaluate programs are feedback meetings that should be held soon after a program is completed to gather timely feedback from program collaborators. I've called these meetings "summing-up sessions," and they are a type of evaluation. These types of meetings are commonly used to gather information about the outcomes of programs and are helpful for assessing perceptions of those who were workers on programs. Partners and other program collaborators during these summative evaluation meetings can express their views on what went well and what did not go well. Feedback of this kind can be used to make program improvements. Remember that even a well-run and well-attended program can often be improved. Keep written meeting notes of summative evaluation meetings so that the feedback given can be acted on later as needed.

If something didn't go as well as expected with a program, it's useful to try to determine as soon as possible from feedback any shortcomings or problems so that they can be corrected in future programming efforts. It might be that the venue wasn't a convenient location for a targeted audience, especially for younger audiences that are dependent on parents or public transportation to attend an event. Perhaps the meeting time was inconvenient for a group or groups that were considered the prime audience. Even when the greatest of care is taken during the planning stage for programs, issues may arise during programs that are unforeseen and present unavoidable negative consequences. A weather emergency, for example, can happen that upsets the best-laid plans. On the other hand, constructive criticism should always be viewed as an opportunity to improve the work of a team and to help it move forward.

Lastly, library program coordinators and other program planners should conduct a reflective assessment. This type of assessment is used by programmers as a method of review of the work accomplished as program developers and workers. This helps to build on existing programming practices. It helps individuals to think more introspectively and critically about their program practice or work. How might we as programmers evaluate our efforts in terms of negative and positive outcomes of the program? If a partnership was involved in the programming effort, how would you describe the experience? In what ways can the partnership experience be improved? What might we do differently next time to improve the program and increase participant involvement and satisfaction in the program?

GENERAL RULES IN CONDUCTING ASSESSMENTS

When conducting assessments of programs, it's important to ensure that all evaluations are culturally responsive. A definition of culturally responsive evaluation is provided in a National Science Foundation publication (2002):

> [C]ulturally responsive evaluation attempts to fully describe and explain the context of the program or project being evaluated. Culturally responsive evaluators honor the cultural context in which an evaluation takes place by bringing needed, shared life experience and understanding to the evaluation tasks at hand. (63)

In other words, evaluators should be aware of and sensitive to the lifeways, values, and mores of the cultural groups within the audiences that programs are intended to serve. It is useful to have representatives from the targeted audience population involved in part of the evaluation process. Program volunteers or audience participants, for example, can be invited into the evaluation process. Program volunteers can be invited for a post-program chat (in-person or virtually in Google Hangout or a Zoom meeting) or to a luncheon that is held post-program to provide feedback about the program. In this way, it's possible to find out an insider's perspective about the outcome of the program. Sponsors of programs should be aware that views about programs may be different among different demographic groups.

In my practice of assessing programs that promote African American writers, I've primarily used library program assessments that are based on mixed evaluation methods. Using attendance numbers combined with summaries from follow-up meetings with partners and volunteers to evaluate programs has worked well for me. I sometimes use program surveys or questionnaires. However, I've discovered that program attendees often do not want to take the time to fill out questionnaires, especially if they are lengthy. If you have access to attendees' emails, consider sending program questionnaires to attendees via email to get their feedback.

In general, however, software applications such as SurveyMonkey have made it easier to design and conduct surveys. The app provides a means for persons to take the survey online after attending a program. If surveys are used, it is best to have brief, simplified questionnaires that only take a few minutes to complete.

Library programmers will discover that different assessment tools work best based on the type of program offered and the composition of the audience. Qualitative tools may prove best to determine the value of programs to audience attendees or library users. One librarian, writing on qualitative techniques (focus groups, ethnographic studies, etc.) that are used to evaluate library services, states, "Increasingly, library users are in search of better user experiences—improvements that cannot be communicated via survey or statistical data" (Goodman, 2011, 64). For instance, programs featuring African American writers and writing may provide a haven for African American youth in search of a space where they feel a sense of belonging. Other library users might seek out African American writers and diverse literature programs out of curiosity or for a class assignment. Still others may attend such programs because they already have an appreciation for African American literature. Whatever the motivation, attendees of programs that feature African American writers or writing often find it to be an enjoyable and sometime challenging learning experience.

In conclusion, make a conscious effort to obtain post-program reactions from African American authors who were your featured program guests by asking them about their experience. This is a type of evaluation. Communicating through an email message or a telephone call after your library event or program may result in information that can be added to your program assessment report. Author guests may have interesting stories to tell about their experience and interactions with program audiences. Their impressions or memorable stories about audience engagement or an interaction with an individual audience member may provide a special story to complement your evaluation. In an anecdote from the visit by illustrator AG Ford at one of the AARI programs, I was told that a young boy from an elementary school was so impressed after reading some of the books that Ford illustrated and after watching Ford demonstrate drawing, he drew a portrait of Ford to give to him as a gift. Brief stories or anecdotes such as this can provide qualitative evidence that your program made a positive impression.

Often authors or a publisher representative may arrange for the sale of books at your program venues. Be sure to get information on the number of books sold, book-signing photos, and descriptions of any interesting incidents that happen. In fact, have a designated photographer from your own program team assigned to take photos, not only during book signings, but throughout the programs. A good photographer is a great asset to programmers. Photos provide excellent visual documentation to include as part of an assessment report.

PURPOSES AND USES OF ASSESSMENT

After the hard and often exhausting work of planning and putting on a library program, don't neglect the important task of completing a written and documented assessment of the program itself! It is very important! The purpose of the assessment as stated earlier is to evaluate—hopefully—the positive impact or influence of a planned public entertainment event or learning event on an audience. It's important to report how the program affected or influenced the people that made up the audience. Even if you just report the number of persons who attended the program, this shows quantitatively that people cared enough or were motivated enough to show up! Other items that might be included in the final assessment are the results of questionnaires completed by program attendees, some positive participant quotations, photographs of the event, and a list of media reviews of the program with some positive excerpts.

With whom should evaluations be shared? A record of the event and an assessment of it should be shared with one's supervisor or supervisors, program cosponsors, and other program stakeholders. This will provide evidence for them that is advantageous to gaining continued or even greater organizational support and funding of programs. Furthermore, it's beneficial to have a record of past successful programming so that it can be used as evidence of competencies when applying for grant support for programs that you might desire to put on in the future.

If the program sponsorship comes from a library, a brief report can be shared with librarian colleagues in your city or state through newsletters. Make sure to give written assessment reports to institutional administrators such as school principals, public library directors, and university library deans. A summary of the report might be made available generally within the organization in the form of a short article in an organization's newsletter or on their website.

Library programs that promote African American writers that garner positive pubic response and high audience participation can leave a positive, lasting influence on library users. Successful library programs that have positive impact on individuals within communities help to build the reputation of the library. Individuals who attend quality programming carry the news of their positive experiences about the library out to others in the community. This helps to build the reputation of the library as an inviting and helpful place. The opposite might be true if library patrons have a negative experience. Guard against making a bad impression. If library programs are viewed as positive, this grows collective support for libraries and persuades once non-users of libraries to become library patrons. Library programming builds good public opinion about libraries as social institutions, as places that support community engagement and healthy communities.

Assessment of library programming can provide evidence of patron support for library programming. On the one hand, it may point up areas where improvements are needed. In most cases these improvements or changes can be easily made. Satisfied patrons are what libraries want and need for sustainability. It's a means to show accountability to supervisors. Assessment of library programming helps librarians to stay aware of some perceptions about the library and its programs. Library users who actively attend library programs are more likely to draw others such as their friends and family to the library, which adds to the vitality of libraries. And these patrons are more likely to become financial supporters of libraries.

When programs are finished and after assessments are "wrapped up" as part of the final assessment phase, it's a good time to start some preliminary brainstorming of ideas for programs that might be tried in the future or ways to make corrections in some areas that did not go well. Programmers should always have an eye toward improving programs for the future. Ideas and feedback from summative evaluations can be folded into a program assessment final report.

SUMMARY

This chapter provides a general definition for assessment. Assessment is an evaluation of impact or effect of a planned event, program, or service on library users or potential users. The chapter provides examples of assessments that use quantitative and qualitative techniques to assess or evaluate programs that promote African American writers. General guidelines and purposes are given for doing good program assessments.

In the next chapter, I encourage programming leaders and other program planners to conduct a reflective assessment of their work. The latter type of assessment is used by programmers as a method to thoroughly examine existing programming practices more introspectively and critically. How might program planners critically evaluate their program outcomes? What might programmers do differently as individuals and collectively, to improve their work in developing programs? These and other questions will be addressed in the next chapter.

REFERENCES

American Library Association. "Core Values of Librarianship." American Library Association, July 26, 2006. http://www.ala.org/advocacy/intfreedom/corevalues. Accessed April 29, 2022.

Coleman, Mary Catherine. *Shared Foundations: Collaborate.* Chicago: ALA Edition, American Association of School Librarians, 2020.

Frierson, Henry T., Stafford Hood, and Gerunda B. Hughes. "Strategies That Address Culturally Responsive Evaluation." In *The 2002 User-Friendly Handbook for Project Evaluation.* National Science Foundation, 63–73. https://www.nsf.gov /pubs/2002/nsf02057/nsf02057.pdf. Accessed June 5, 2022.

Goodman, Valeda Dent. *Qualitative Research and the Modern Library.* Cambridge, UK: Chandos Publishing, 2011.

6

Reflective and Intentional Programming to Promote African American Writers

INTRODUCTION

We have explored how to promote African American writers by using innovative programming ideas and by working with new and sometime unexpected partners. This exploration happened while examining case examples of programming from a wide variety of libraries. Furthermore, various assessment techniques to evaluate programs were provided. However, two areas that were not talked about much are reflectivity and intentionality. What is reflectivity? What is intentionality? How are reflectivity and intentionality important to doing programming? And how may they be used to develop programs that promote African American writers?

In this chapter, I first define "reflectivity" and "intentionality" using library literature and other scholarly sources. I then show on a practical level how these concepts can be used by librarians, providing concrete examples that illustrate how they were used in the past by programmers for the promotion of African American writers.

Secondly, I reflect on the confluence of three interrelated areas that, I believe, impact the promotion of African American writers: publishing, collecting, and programming.

Lastly, I share information about the idea of intentionality. I illustrate this idea with the case example of student library users who became activists at one of the libraries where I was employed. These student activists helped to save the Neal-Marshall Black Culture Center (NMBCC) Library at Indiana University.

DEFINITIONS OF REFLECTIVITY AND INTENTIONALITY

Most of us reflect on our lives and daily activities. We might reflect on what went well during our day or what went badly. Reflectivity is a term arising from the fields of psychology and education (Dewey, 1933). John Dewey, a philosopher and founder of pragmatism, was a pioneer in both education and functional psychology. He promoted learning by doing, which is related to reflectivity. In fact, reflectivity refers to an individual's ability to think and to practice introspection and self-examination. It is a practice used by both teachers and librarians.

Reflectivity was mentioned in the previous chapter on assessment in relation to summative evaluation meetings to discuss the impact of programs. Program coordinators and program workers, generally, can use reflection to improve their programming by critically examining their activities. Reflective practice or reflectivity is the ability to think about one's actions and make adjustments when needed as part of a process of continuous growth. Successful program developers reflect on their practice and critically evaluate their actions. This helps them to assess, correct problems, and build on successes. Reflection, in addition, helps people to embrace new ideas or ways of doing things. Programs, especially ones that are recurring, must show dynamism. If they don't, they will fizzle out and die or fall flat. Strong, excellent programmers always look for ways to be innovative in developing programs. In many ways, programmers must be like good entertainers who keep audiences' attention, keep audiences coming back for more, and keep attracting new, expanding audiences.

People learn by doing or through reflective practice. The same is true of those who develop programs to promote African American writers. There is a process of trying new program ideas for audience response. According to Dewey's pragmatic philosophy,

> To "learn from experience" is to make a backward and forward connection between what we do to things and what we enjoy or suffer from things in consequence. Under such conditions, doing becomes a trying; an experiment with the world to find out what it is like; undergoing becomes instruction—discovery of the connection of things. (ibid., 76)

Teachers use reflection to improve their teaching. In fact, reflection is applied as a process of continuing education or action research that is used by both seasoned and beginning teachers. Likewise, librarians and others can use reflection to improve their programming. Librarians and other programmers can adopt this practice, as described by one expert who has studied reflection:

> Teachers reflect on what they are doing and what is going on in their classrooms in order to engage in some direct action to improve the conditions of

learning. Often problem-solving strategies are used. Prospective teachers are helped in defining and redefining problems they want to address. They then determine what kinds of information would help them understand their problems better and how to collect that information. They generate various ideas for changing the situation, decide what actions to undertake, justify those actions according to sound criteria, and evaluate their actions and decision-making process. (Villa, 1997, 82)

Librarians and other programmers can adopt these same strategies to improve their programming.

"Intentionality" is a concept term with origins in philosophy. It relates to the mindfulness that directs an individual's actions. Philosophers have debated the concept over centuries, and as described by one scholar, "One of the ways that philosophers have explained what they mean by 'intentionality' is this: it is that aspect of mental states or events that consists in their being *of* or *about* things . . ." (Siewert, 2017). In the specialization area of promotion of African American writers and their writing discussed in this book, proactive program planners are *about* looking for opportunities to promote African American authors. These planners are ready advocates *of* these programs.

Librarians and others who are involved in program planning to promote African American writers can learn from the philosophy of intentionality and mindfulness. In relation to this book, program planners should ask themselves, "Am I providing programming for the public good that substantially promotes African American writers and their works?"

USES OF REFLECTIVITY AND INTENTIONALITY FOR LIBRARIANS

I've mentioned how reflectivity and intentionality are commonly used in the field of education for teaching and learning. Let's examine how these concepts are applied in library programming for the promotion of African American writers using some examples from library literature and from my own experiences.

Librarians in their professional practice for instruction use reflection and intentionality. They can do the same when they are developing programs that promote African American writers. For example, Graf and Harris (2016) published a journal article about the results of their exploratory study in which they examined how a group of librarians use reflective assessment in their evaluation of individual library instruction and in their library instruction programs. They found that reflectivity is useful not only to individual library instructors for self-introspection, but also when librarians come together as a group for critical assessment. They assert,

> Our experience also confirms the advice of Linda Valli, who has researched reflective practice among teachers. Valli . . . notes that "because reflection is not an end in itself, but for the purpose of action, communal dialogue is essential." For all its introspective connotations, self-reflection cannot be individually determined and realized; it is transformative through engagement. (Graf and Harris, 2016, 42)

To promote African American writers, librarians will find it useful to practice reflection and intentionality. An area in which many practicing librarians utilize reflection is in their pursuit of continuing education in areas that they feel need improvement. Likewise, programming librarians can use continuing education to update their professional skills and knowledge for program preparation and development. Librarians who design programs for the promotion of African American writers and other diverse writers can use training and continuing education designed to intentionally improve their promotion skills in areas such as interpersonal communication, community engagement, and marketing.

A group of leading national researchers brought together by the American Libraries Association derived a list of nine programming competencies for library coordinators of library programs, which was published in a 2019 report, *National Impact of Library Public Program Assessment: Phase 1* (NILPPA) (Sheppard, 2019, 12). See the chart of NILPPA competencies in this chapter. The competencies include a range of attributes from knowledge of community to event planning and financial accounting skills.

On the other hand, I believe that developing successful educational and cultural library programs is seldom the work of one person. Programming requires group effort organizationally, dialogue, and agreement on actions. Additionally, one single individual may not excel in, or even possess, all nine of the identified programming competencies. Educational and cultural programming and other successful library programs require the involvement of many persons and at many different levels of an organization. Programs need "buy-in" or support from everyone in a library from directors to front-line staffers to make programs successful.

An example of a skill or competency that program coordinators must have is the ability to navigate organizational protocols to build institutional support. As a coordinator for programs that promote African American writers, I've found that it was often necessary to follow intricate lines of protocol to make cultural programs happen, but also to be willing and able to be a strong advocate for equity, diversity, and inclusion (EDI) within organizations and institutions and to recruit like-minded persons.

Program coordinators must take an honest inventory of their own abilities and be willing, as well, to recruit committee members or volunteers who can bring different skill sets, perspectives, and knowledge to the table to form a winning team for developing successful programming. I have found that educational and cultural programs are most successful when persons work together to build partnerships and achieve participants' and stakeholders' "buy-in." In fact, stakeholders may encompass both those who are organizers of the programs and recipients of program content.

What do you, the readers of this book, believe to be your strengths as a programmer based on the nine competencies of programming librarians found in the NILPPA study?

The Nine Competencies of Programming Librarians

- Organizational Skills
- Knowledge of Community
- Interpersonal Skills
- Event Planning
- Creativity
- Content Knowledge
- Outreach and Marketing
- Financial Skills
- Evaluation

Michelle Reale is an academic librarian, teacher, and author of several published books on topics that range from embedded librarianship to mentoring. Reale wrote a book titled *Becoming a Reflective Librarian and Teacher.* She states that its purpose is to "serve as a friendly and informative guide, which is not intended to be exhaustive but instead to start the journey toward reflection" (Reale, 2017, xiv). She defines reflection as a deliberate and intentional thought process that leads to an assessment of how one works. Reale sees reflection and particularly reflective journaling as something that can lead to personal growth. Reale recommends that librarians keep a reflective journal as a tool to professional development and personal growth. In her book she provides concrete examples from her own journaling about everything from her personal life to her professional career experiences as a teacher and a librarian. Through her journal examples, scholarly literature references, and recommended strategies she provides a guide that programmers will find helpful in accomplishing their goals.

Journaling clears and relaxes the mind, like other good health habits such as nutritious eating and physical exercise and getting sufficient sleep. Coordinating and organizing programs are stressful. Embracing philosophies of reflectivity and intentionality are mindful exercises that have grounded me to think strategically and approach forthrightly my identity as an academic librarian with a passion for programming that promotes African American writers.

Academic librarianship has changed, but programming, for a large part of my career, was seen in the library profession as a specialization of public libraries. According to the Public Libraries Survey conducted in 2016 by the Institute of Museum and Library Services, public libraries increased their sponsorship of programs by 72.1 percent between 2010 and 2016 to 5.2 million programs presented across the United States. The survey found, "The trend toward increased programming continues in libraries of all types, including public libraries, academic and school libraries, and a host of special libraries" (Sheppard et al., 2019, 4).

The misconception that public programs are appropriate only to public libraries is something that I've intentionally addressed while negotiating my path as an academic librarian. While at Indiana University (IU), it was helpful to have a librarian liaison role with the African American and African Diaspora Studies Department and to be physically based within the cultural center with the African American Arts Institute and the Theatre Department. The latter made my involvement in presenting educational cultural programs to promote African American writers and other academic support programs appear to be a natural fit. In a second academic setting, at Missouri State University, I philosophically positioned myself with the Public Affairs Mission of the university, which includes the three pillar areas of cultural competence, community engagement, and ethical leadership. I consciously designed my research and programming work to fit the standards for engaged public scholarship.

My advice to all academic librarians who have a passion for programming is to think intentionally. If your institution provides promotion and tenure for librarians or other types of career promotion, be informed and knowledgeable of all its policies and guidelines. Begin early to circumspectly plan your professional career goals around the policies and strategic goals of the institution where you work.

What is intentional library programming? Intentionality in librarianship, whether it be around the area of developing programs, buying materials for collections, or teaching literacy instruction, is about activity that is focused and purposeful. One librarian writes, "Diversifying our collections and programs requires intentionality. It requires librarians and staff intentionally taking the time, when designing programs and creating booklists, to ask: 'Who is missing?' 'Who haven't we seen in the library?' and 'What other perspectives can we bring to this program?'" (Africa Hands, 2015, 19).

While a librarian at the IU Neal-Marshall Black Culture Center (NMBCC), much of my programming focused on themes and services for incoming freshman and undergraduate students generally. Programs were developed around student recruitment and retention, for example, to help first-generation students entering college through preparation programs such as Upward Bound and what was known at IU as the "Groups Program." The library that I directed in the Neal-Marshall Black Culture Center helped these students to feel welcomed and supported. Students were involved in choosing books for the library collection and in deciding what authors to invite to speak through a student advisory board and other mechanisms for user input. Program planning included special receptions, library orientations, tours for the Groups Program, and displays that featured photographs of cohorts of students engaged in library activities.

During most of my years as a librarian at Missouri State University (MSU), my primary library responsibilities were in the areas of teaching librarianship for prospective library and information science students who were part of a partnership program between MSU in Springfield and the University of Missouri in Columbia or in teaching information literacy skills to undergraduates. In this teaching librarianship role, I had time set aside to do my own research that was often focused on public service scholarship. My service work was designed prominently around my coordinator duties as chairperson of the Springfield African American Read-In (AARI). I designed programs to provide learning opportunities and service projects for MSU students, as well as students from other local college campuses and for high school and middle school students who lived in the communities surrounding the college campuses. Whenever possible, I utilized MSU facilities as the venue to hold programs, which made the programs accessible to MSU students while at the same time providing a special "field-trip" type experience for area high school and middle school students or a special event atmosphere for others who live in the community around the university campus.

An example of intentional programming is found in the library literature in a study of a book advisory group for children (Fullerton et al., 2018). An analysis by experts in librarianship who were making picture book recommendations for children's literature and rationales for read-alouds (109 recommendations with 95 unique titles) shows the influence of their decision-making. The librarians recommended a balance in terms of having books with characters of color and different genders, but fewer books were selected that had authors or illustrators of color. The study's researchers acknowledged that part of this disparity could be related to the fact that publishers are not keeping up with public demand and need for diversity in children's literature. Part of the solution, therefore, is to have more books for children and youth that are written by African American authors come through publishing pipelines so that librarians and other programmers can highlight these works to the public through programs.

For more than thirty years, publishing statistics on children's and young adult books have been documented by the Cooperative Children's Book Center (CCBC) at the School of Education, University of Wisconsin-Madison. Statistics over the decades consistently show a low level of publishing of books about African American characters or other people of color including Latinx, Asian/Asian Americans, and First/Native Nations. In 2018, the CCBC found that of the 3,312 children's books published and

TABLE 6-1. Children's Books by and/or about People of Color and First/Native Nations Received by the CCBC—U.S. Publishers Only, 2018–2021

Year	Books Received at CCBC (US Pubs)	Black/African		Indigenous		Asian		Latinx		Pacific Islanders		Arab	
		By	About	By	About	By	About	By	About	By	About	By	About
2021	3,183*	306	438	47	61	464	338	311	234	8	6	21	21
2020	3,260*	256	400	27	41	387	310	230	195	1	5	17	22
2019	3,751	227	459	31	45	393	336	237	235	5	5	19	33
2018	3,352	205	389	27	34	358	309	208	243	2	6	15	24

Data on books by and about Black, Indigenous, and People of Color published for children and teens compiled by the Cooperative Children's Book Center, School of Education, University of Wisconsin-Madison. Reprinted with permission. Available online at https://ccbc .education.wisc.edu/literature-resources/ccbc-diversity-statistics/books-by-and-or-about-poc -2018/#Usonly. (Last updated April 6, 2022.)

received by the center that year, only 388 (11.71 percent) were about African Americans. Furthermore, African American authors were responsible for a little less than half of the published books about African Americans that year. The question then arises, "Who is best suited to tell the story of a people and a culture?" The CCBC's research shows that primarily the stories involving people of color or characters representing African Americans, Latinx, Asian/Asian Americans, and First/Native Nations are told by authors whose lived experience is outside those cultures or authors who are White/Caucasian. Table 6-1 is compiled from CCBC data that shows publication statistics of books by authors of color and about people of color.

National School Library Standards require that school librarians be intentional in engaging students by using four domain areas: Think, Create, Share, and Grow. When developing school library collections and programs, school librarians must exercise equity, diversity, and inclusion (EDI). National standards require that diverse collections be made available in all school libraries. This requires intentional collection development policies and purchases that include African American authors and other authors of color. In addition, school librarians should work in partnership with classroom teachers as well as students to develop collections and programs. In some schools, past enrollments had few students of color, but due to changes in population growth in many areas, demographic shifts have occurred, and there are presently a significant number of enrolled students of color. The demographic composition of student populations in schools across the United States has changed, along with reading tastes.

THREE INTERLOCKING AREAS: PUBLISHING, COLLECTING, AND PROGRAMMING

There are three interlocking areas that affect the promotion of African American writers: publishing, collecting, and programming. In this section, I will reflect on how promotion of African American writers is influenced by these factors.

Publishers play a vital role in the pipeline that provides access to books by African American writers and other People of Color. The more published books by African American writers, the more choices of works there are available for the development of cultural and educational programs. To address the former need and the disparity in publishing of writers of color, more librarians, teachers, and other advocates have come forward to advocate for publishing of African American authors and other authors of color.

For instance, in 2020, the nonprofit We Need Diverse Books, which advocates for more diversity in children's literature, took a proactive role to influence the adult book publishing industry. They created two internship grants for persons from diverse backgrounds to help them find mentors in the publishing industry who would be capable of preparing them to work in the adult publishing industry. The five-year-grant was made possible through a donation from author Celeste Ng (Maher, 2020, 5).

In another example of opening publishing to more African American writers and generally promoting more diversity, equity, and inclusion in publishing, Black author L. L. McKinney started the hashtag #PublishingPaidMe that trended on Twitter. She described her hashtag as an outgrowth of conversations with friends about Black and other authors of color "being historically underpaid and underappreciated by the white publishing industry" (Deahl, 2020, 4). As a result of the hashtag, more than two thousand authors revealed advances they received for their books, but it was difficult to prove without more transparency in publishing and sufficient data the inequities that have long been discussed.

In 2019, a survey of public library programming events conducted by PanoramaProject.org found that programming in public libraries contributes tremendously to book discovery, author brand development, and consumer sales (Panorama Project, 2019). The survey covered two hundred libraries in thirty states but did not report on the racial and ethnic background of the authors featured in library programming. It did, however, demonstrate the expansive reach that public libraries have in increasing public awareness about authors to communities through programming. According to the survey's findings, larger libraries that serve populations of one hundred thousand or more (39.5 percent of survey respondents) held multifaceted programming events like author visits and book sales, while the smaller libraries promoted authors on a smaller scale and with a local author dominance. According to the survey,

> Libraries tend to feature authors of all kinds, but traditionally published non-fiction authors are the most common for multi-event libraries, while those producing fewer events are more varied to 90 percent relying on local authors vs. 67 percent for the others. (2019–2020 Libraries Events and Book Sales Survey, PanoramaProgject.org, 12)

To encourage readers of this book to buy more books published by African American and other writers of color, I provide here a list of small press minority publishers. These multifaceted, established small press African American and other minority-owned publishers provide opportunities for African American and other writers of color to be published. They provide unique titles to build programming around.

Africa World Press (Literature on the history, culture, politics of Africa and the African diaspora)
Amistad Press (Founded in 1986, their website states, "to specialize in the works of authors who honor and consecrate the memory of those who fought—and continue to fight—for freedom.")
Black Classic Press (Founded in 1976, their website states, "devoted to publishing obscure and significant works by and about people of African descent.")
BLF Press (Black feminist books)
Just Us Books (Black interest children's books)
Lee & Low Books (Diverse children's books)
Third World Press (Largest independent Black-owned press in the United States focused on culturally progressive and political books of all genre)
Vital Narrative Press (Publishing house of writers of color)
World Stage Press (An extension of World Stage Writers' Workshop for African American Writers)

Banks (1993) and other education scholars who study multicultural education have found positive impacts of diverse literature and multicultural education for children and teens for "prejudice reduction." Quality programming to promote African American authors and multidimensional African American characters or images in literature increases the appreciation of African American culture among all library patrons and readers. Books by African American authors that have positive images of Black culture build self-esteem among African American youth.

Teachers and librarians in K–12 schools, public librarians, and academic librarians alike, by providing diverse collections and programs, help to nurture and educate all of America's youth by showing the diversity of people who make up American society. One way to accomplish this is to support publishers of quality diverse books. However, educators, librarians, and publishers are not always keeping pace with public desires or the societal need for equity, diversity, and inclusion. For instance, 2015 was the first year since 1977 that both the Newberry and the Caldecott Awards that recognize outstanding children's literature went to writers of color—African American Kwame Alexander won the Newberry Medal for *The Crossover* and Asian American Dan Santat won the Caldecott Medal for *The Adventures of Beekle: The Unimaginary Friend.*

Intentional library programmers can take a proactive approach through communication and other means to encourage publishers to publish more books by African American writers and other diverse writers. To ensure quality purchases, librarians and other buyers can look for book reviews in reputable journals and websites to find books by African American writers. Another means to ensure diversity in materials selections is for libraries to establish advisory committees made up of library patrons of diverse backgrounds. Librarians can make a concerted effort to discover patrons' favorite authors. Additionally, before making book purchases, one can seek the advice of K–12 teachers and college faculty members who teach literature, history, or other courses who are knowledgeable about African American writers and other ethnic and racially diverse writers to ask their views on titles.

At library conferences, I make a conscious effort to peruse exhibits and to visit with small press publishers, as well as the large publishers who regularly publish writers of color. I purchase from publishers of diverse books and thank those who demonstrate support of EDI.

Programmers must be proactive in developing good intraorganizational, working relationships with library collection departments. Programmers can then provide input for new books published by African American authors and other writers of color to librarian colleagues in collection development departments or other designated intraorganizational areas that are responsible for collecting resource materials. Intentional programmers should take an active role in recommending and advocating for the collecting of books by African American writers and other diverse authors. Intentional library programmers then follow-up their libraries' purchases by taking advantage of some of the best new writing that is purchased by their libraries to design programming around the titles and their authors. These programs can draw more patrons into the library made up of interested faculty, students, staff, and community members who want to learn about the titles written by African American writers and to read them.

SPECIAL COLLECTIONS AND ARCHIVES AND THE INTENTIONAL PROMOTION OF AFRICAN AMERICAN WRITERS

Developing special collections of local or regional African American community materials is another act of intentionality in diversity library services that is bringing recognition to African American writers, oral histories, and

historical artifacts. The former types of collections offer opportunities of
foci on which to develop programming! An exemplary project of this type is
the locally planned and developed archive for the historical Crispus Attucks
High School in Indianapolis. The school was the first high school for African
American students built in the city in 1927, during a period of segregation.
The Crispus Attucks High School archival collection was created through a
partnership involving the Crispus Attucks Museum, Indiana University and
Purdue University at Indianapolis (IUPUI) Libraries and various other community organizations (Cruz, 2019, 223). This collection preserves copies of
the student newspaper and student yearbooks among other materials.

At MSU, the late faculty member Katherine Lederer, in cooperation with
citizens of the Springfield African American community, brought together
approximately seventy-five hundred documents over twenty years. It is now
known as the Lederer Collection. MSU Libraries received the collection as a
donation in the year 2000 and is helping to preserve and further develop it.
Much of the collection spans the nineteenth century. A part of the collection
was created into an exhibit and shown in 1986 titled *Many Thousands
Gone: Springfield's Lost Black History*. The exhibit was digitized and is now
available for research and public program use through *Umbra Search African American History*. Umbra is a freely available Internet search tool
(www.umbrasearch.org) that makes the Lederer Collection and many other
like collections available to a wide public audience.

The University of Minnesota Libraries developed a partnership with the
Penumbra Theatre Company, which launched Umbra in 2012. The digital
platform was developed using grants from the Institute of Museum and
Library Services (IMLS) and the Doris Duke Charitable Foundation, in
addition to assistance from the Council on Library and Information
Resources. Through national partners, Umbra brings together more than
500,000 digitized materials from over one thousand libraries, archives, and
cultural heritage institutions across the United States. Some of the larger
institutional Umbra partners include Yale University, Temple University,
Howard University, and the Smithsonian Institution. Umbra sponsors
research, educational programs, and fellowships. It is a treasure trove of
materials for program developers.

In conjunction with developing intentional programming around physically accessible, local African American history collections and archives,
librarians and other programmers can find and use complementary digital
materials using search tools like Umbra. Another internet resource available
for exploring and researching are the digitized collections of the Archives
Library Information Center (ALIC). The ALIC is part of the National
Archives of the United States. The purpose of the ALIC is to provide government staff and researchers access to background information available in
the National Archives and Records Administration. An excellent compen-
dium of national, state, regional, and local resources on Black history can be

found on the ALIC website (https://www.archives.gov/research/alic/reference
/black-history.html).

STUDENTS PROTESTS SAVE A UNIVERSITY LIBRARY

At the beginning of this book, I explained how my love of library programming began at Indiana University (IU) with my position as director of
the library that was part of the Neal-Marshall Black Culture Center
(NMBCC). Little did I expect that after four short years into that position
as head of that brand new, small, and unique library that it would be threatened with closure and having its doors locked forever. But that is exactly
what happened.

After the grand opening of the Neal-Marshall Black Culture Center and Theatre and Drama Center complex, the library got off to a good start with programs and services. The library developed a partnership with the Drama Center
to house their script collection, which provided more efficient borrowing access
for students and instructors. The library partnered with other parts of the
NMBCC and with different IU academic departments in hosting book talks,
interdepartmental exhibits, and several annual Evening Extravaganza Dinners
featuring faculty author guest speakers. All events and programs were free and
open to the public. Thousands of IU's students, faculty, and staff, along with
persons from the larger community, utilized our services and physical collections. But it was not enough when IU Libraries Administration compared it to
IU's main library that was housed in its eleven-floor limestone structure.

The IU Libraries Administration had given verbal warnings and made
threatening overtures that the library in the NMBCC, if its circulation of
materials or gate count of users did not increase, could be closed. Numbers
did increase to show improvement during the library's early years. Furthermore, I advocated vehemently for the library as a hub for open dialogue and
engagement for students. African American students especially gained a
sense of belonging there in the library's cultural space, on a predominantly
White institution (PWI) campus where African American students made up
about 3 percent of the student population that numbered about twenty-four
thousand at the time I was there.

Nevertheless, during a final examination period toward the end of a
spring semester, students heard through leaks that university administrators
and IU Libraries Administration were planning to permanently close the
library in the NMBCC at the end of the semester. Without my knowledge,
the students swung into action and mobilized with an intentional plan to
not allow the library closure. In the span of three days, starting in the middle
of final exam week, the students executed their plan of protests and presented their demands to IU administrators that the library that they identified with and used not be closed. They demanded a meeting with the dean
of IU Libraries and spoke before the IU Board of Trustees.

An outline of the students' intentional protests and plans was documented in several articles in the IU student newspaper, *Indiana Daily Student*, and the local city newspaper, *The Herald-Times*. The students' actions occurred from Wednesday, May 3, 2006, through May 5, 2006, as reported in the news articles. See excerpts from two of the news articles in this chapter. The lead story with photograph on the front page of *The Herald-Times*, "Students Rally to Save Library at Neal-Marshall Center," by Sarah Morin, reports the successful result of the student protests (see Figure 6-1).

Student leaders outraged by news that IU was closing the library at the Neal-Marshall Black Culture Center mobilized a campaign Wednesday to save it.

FIGURE 6-1. "Students Rally to Save Library at Neal-Marshall Center," *The Herald Times,* May 4, 2006.

Copyright © The Herald-Times—USA TODAY NETWORK. Reprinted with permission. Available online at https://www.heraldtimesonline.com/story/news/2006/05/04/studentsrally-to-save-library-at-neal-marshall-center/117850164/.

It worked.

Library administrators decided not to close the library after meeting with 40 or so concerned Indiana University students. (Morin, 2006, 1)

"Before the meeting [with library administrators], students had stayed overnight in the library to create a plan to save it . . . [and they decided to] lead a march at noon Wednesday from the Neal-Marshall Black Culture Center (NMBCC) to the main Wells Library" (Morin, 2006, 1). During the march of nearly one hundred, students carried armloads of books that they had checked out from the library in the NMBCC and "poster board signs that read: 'Last to come, first to go' and 'Now our library, next our rights'" (Morin, ibid.). Students had written a letter to Interim Library Dean Pat Steele and created a petition that contained the names of 250 students and some faculty members that they delivered to the dean with a demand to keep open the library at the NMBCC.

Students had begun congregating at the library in the NMBCC to talk about what they viewed as a crisis situation and to develop a course of action on Wednesday, May 3, 2006, according to a news article that appeared in the *Indiana Daily Student*, May 5, 2006, by Carrie Ritchie (see Figure 6-2) (Ritchie, 2006). The intentional student protest was carried out through a partnership of leadership between the IU Black Student Union and the IU

Indiana Daily Student

2
FRIDAY
MAY 5, 2006

CAMPUS

www.idsnews.com

Campus Editors:
Trevor Brown
brownt@indiana.edu

Students protest AACC library closing

By Carrie Ritchie
ccritch@indiana.edu

More than 70 students and staff gathered in the African American Cultural Center Library in the Neal-Marshall Black Cultural Center shortly after 11:30 a.m. Wednesday to make signs and check out books to protest the closing of the library they cherish as a symbol of their culture.

As they knelt around tables sharing big black markers to write slogans on red, yellow and green posters, outgoing Black Student Union President Courtney Williams encouraged students to fight back to protect their "hub."

The students had found out only the night before that their library wasn't just going to close for the summer, it was going to close permanently. Within hours, they organized a sit-in and a protest. Fifty students spent the night in the library as part of the sit-in and made signs for the protests during breaks they took from studying for finals. They also created a petition that many students and faculty signed as they filed into the library to prepare for the protest.

"The big thing is we can't have a cultural center without books," said junior Grace Akinlemibola as she signed the petition. "We need books to have a culture. If you take the library away, what else can you take away?" Deha Alexander, a graduate stu-

dent, was especially upset because she said she used the library to hold office hours and meet with students.

"I'm in this library a lot and I want to come out and make it known how angry I am, not just at them closing the library, but the sneaky way they did it," Alexander said. "We're taking the time away from our papers and studying and we're here to let the University know that whatever criteria they used to determine whether the library is valuable to students, they didn't use the right criteria."

The students said that one of the biggest causes of their frustration was that the library didn't receive the same technology updates as other libraries. They think that better technology would improve the facility and encourage more students of all races to use the library.

Senior Megan Selby, an education reform major, was upset because she said the library has so much value and IU claims to have a commitment to diversity, yet the University doesn't promote the facility.

"Instead of shutting it down, IU's response should be to get the word out about it," she said.

At 12:15 p.m., the protesters filed out the door waving the signs which said things like "Last to come, first to go" and "Black people don't just shoot hoops, we also read." A few were still in their pajamas from the night before.

As they marched up Jordan Avenue to the main entrance of the Herman B Wells Library, they carried stacks of books they checked out but refused to return and chanted "Shut us down, shut us up, shut us down – no way!" Several cars honked their horns in support and some even pulled over to ask about the protest. The group stayed at the library protesting and talking to library administration until around 1 p.m., according to African Students Association President Viviane Saleh-Hanna. She said that by that time, they had 100 supporters and 250 signatures on their petition.

Saleh-Hanna said that library administration promised not to close the library until the end of the 2006-2007 school year. Williams went to the IU Board of Trustees' meeting Thursday and talked to them about admissions standards, tuition increase and the library protest.

"This generated a conversation with the board of trustee members regarding our fight to keep the black cultural center library open," Williams said in an e-mail. "Provost (Michael) McRobbie stated in this meeting that the library in question will not be closing. He also acknowledged that NMBCC library is in a unique situation, and that there needs to be a matter standards in how we evaluate the 'success' of this library; adding that we need to include qualitative and

quantitative evaluations."

Saleh-Hanna said that they view yesterday as a starting point to improve the facilities. She said they would like to add "updated computers with new software, new printers, more books and a reference collection that reflects current research on race, class, nation and politics." She also said that the group appreciated the understanding Roth Lilly Interim Dean of University Libraries Patricia Steele gave them.

"We did appreciate the amount of time Dean Steele spent in discussion with us," she said in an e-mail. "We also appreciate that she has agreed not to close the library down during her term as Dean. We understand that there is more work to be done in regards to the relationship between black students and the IU administration, (but) her decision is reflective of a higher level of open-mindedness."

Steele, in turn, said that she had learned from the students' demonstration. She said she realized that the students had formed an emotional attachment to the library and was happy that they cared so much to protest.

"What I learned is that I can look at it from our cultural view and make assumptions that are not right," she said. "That library is an intellectual symbol and a refuge for those students I can't stand in their shoes, but I got a glimpse of the caring and desire they have for that intellectual space."

Sophomore Sarah Taylor checked out as many books as she could carry to protest the closing of the Neal-Marshall Black Culture Center's Library Wednesday afternoon.

RONNI MOORE • IDS

FIGURE 6-2. "Students Protest AACC Library Closing," *Indiana Daily Student*, May 5, 2006.

African Student Union with support of other IU students and some faculty and staff. On Thursday of that week, the president of the Black Student Union, Courtney Williams, and the president of the African Student Association, Viviane Saleh-Hanna, spoke at a meeting of the IU Board of Trustees about admissions standards, tuition increases, and the threatened closing of the library at the NMBCC, according to the *IDS* article.

SUMMARY

This chapter provides definitions and illustrative examples from library and education literature on the concepts of reflectivity and intentionality. I share personal experiences of how I use reflection and intention in my professional career development, as well as for the goal of promoting African American writers and other diverse writers. I provide news documentation of student protests that saved the library where I was employed at IU.

Two growing areas of intentional collection development in libraries are collecting diverse books and developing special collections of unique materials. In this chapter, I cover these areas with examples of reviewing journals and small press publishers that are helpful resources to finding diverse books to collect and promote. In the area of unique, local special collections, I provide the example of the Crispus Attucks High School Museum and archival collection in Indianapolis and the MSU, Duane G, Meyer Library, Kathern Lederer Collection of Ozarks African American community history. National resources to research African American writers and history were noted with the internet tools *Umbra Search African American History* from the University of Minnesota, and the Archives Library Information Center available through the National Archives of the United States.

In summary, this chapter illustrates how library programmers who are reflective thinkers and intentional actors in their passion to promote African American writers and literature are more likely to grow as leaders, to set goals that are achievable, and to produce programs that are impactful.

It has taken me a whole career to realize some of the important ideas that I've written about in this book and to draw lessons from them. As I look back, I see that some good was accomplished, which makes me very happy and very grateful.

REFERENCES

Africa Hands. "Intentional Diversity: Program Ideas from the Field." *Children &
    Libraries: The Journal of the Association for Library Services to Children* 13,
    no. 3 (2015): 19–22.
Banks, James A. "Multicultural Education: Historical Development, Dimensions,
    and Practice." In *Review of Research in Education*. Edited by L. D. Hammond.
    Washington, DC: American Educational Association, 1993, 3–49.

Cooperative Children's Book Center. "Data on Books by and about People of Color and from First/Native Nations Published for Children and Teens." Cooperative Children's Book Center, School of Education, University of Wisconsin-Madison. https://ccbc.education.wisc.edu/book/pcstats.asp

Cruz, Alice M. "Intentional Integration of Diversity Ideals in Academic Libraries: A Literature Review." *Journal of Academic Librarianship* 45, no. 3 (2019): 220–227.

Deahl, Rachel. July 13, 2020. "#PublishingPaidMe Exposes Racial Inequities." *Publishers Weekly* 267, no. 28: 4–10.

Dewey, John. *How We Think: A Restatement of the Relation of Reflective Thinking to the Educational Process*. Lexington, MA: Heath, 1933.

Fullerton, Susan King, George Schafer, Koti Hubbard, Erin L. McClure, Leslie Sally, and Rachael Ross. "Considering Quality and Diversity: An Analysis of Read-Aloud Recommendations and Rationales from Children's Literature Experts." *New Review of Children's Literature & Librarianship* 24, no. 1 (2018): 76–95.

Graf, Anne Jumonville, and Benjamin R. Harris. "Reflective Assessment: Opportunities and Challenges." *Reference Services Review* 44, no. 1 (2016): 38–47.

Maher, John. (June 1, 2020). "Authors Fight for Diversity." *Publishers Weekly* 267 (22): 5–10.

Morin, Sarah. "Students Rally to Save Library at Neal-Marshall Center." *The Herald-Times* (May 4, 2006): 1.

Panorama Project. "Public Library Events and Book Sales Survey." PanoramaProject.org, 2019. Accessed July 23, 2020.

National Research Council. *Knowing What Students Know: The Science and Design of Educational Assessment*. Washington, DC: National Academy Press, 2001.

Reale, Michelle. *Becoming a Reflective Librarian and Teacher: Strategies for Mindful Academic Practice*. Chicago: American Library Association, 2017.

Ritchie, Carrie. "Students Protest AACC Library Closing." *Indiana Daily Student* (May 5, 2006): 2.

Sheppard, B., K. Flinner, R. J. Norlander, and M. D. Fournier. "National Impact of Library Public Programs Assessment: Phase I." Chicago: American Library Association & New Knowledge Organization, 2019, 12. https://nilppa.org/wp-content/uploads/2019/06/NILPPA_Phase-1-white-paper.pdf. Accessed July 6, 2022.

Siewert, Charles, "Consciousness and Intentionality." In *The Stanford Encyclopedia of Philosophy*. Edited by Edward N. Zalta, Summer 2022 edition. https://plato.standford.edu/archives/sum2022/entries/consciousness-intentionality/

Villa, Linda. "Listening to Other Voices: A Description of Teacher Reflection in the United States." *Peabody Journal of Education* 72, no. 1 (1997): 67–88.

Conclusion

Strong, competent, and energized library programmers must take the lead in disseminating information about their intentional diversity programming. This point is illustrated by Cruz in a journal article on "intentional programming" in which she reviews the literature on "diversity ideals in academic librarianship" (Cruz, 2019, 225–226). In the literature review, Cruz found diversity in areas of staffing, collections, services, and programming, and concluded, "the work of achieving diversity in libraries is far from finished. It is essential that librarians continue to share successful and innovative strategies for integrating diversity into library work via research and publication" (ibid., 226). Cruz's article was in response to the passage of the American College and Research Libraries (ACRL) 2018 Plan for Excellence on Equity, Diversity, and Inclusion.

During most of 2020, throughout 2021, and parts of 2022, American libraries went through years of learning to live with a global pandemic, as well as a national "racial awakening" after the police murder of George Floyd. These traumas and other social factors forced the American Library Association (ALA) to do deeper professional introspection to strengthen its resolve and commitments to equity, diversity, and inclusion (EDI). I believe that promoting African American writers for the reasons outlined in this book is a step in the right direction to pragmatically strengthening libraries' EDI commitment.

LIBRARY TRENDS AND CHALLENGES

Cultural and educational programming is a big trendsetter in libraries. Libraries are no longer only where patrons come to borrow books and to read. Modern libraries are where members of communities come to be engaged—to gather with others and be inspired, to discuss topics in groups, to be informed, and to play and be entertained. When libraries bring authors, poets, spoken word artists, theatre performers, musicians, and more into the library, this makes it a more engaging place that will attract more community members. When they become intentional in promoting African American writers, libraries as cultural institutions will be involved in doing all the latter.

There are many areas of programming that libraries should pursue more vigorously. Programming around African American writers and their writing and other diverse literature should be "top of the list" in programming pursuits. Programming that promotes African American writers and of diverse literature generally is integral to libraries' public missions. It is this programming that is vibrant and that appeals to the growing diverse youth populations in the United States. Offering this programing will help to build overarching healthier and happier communities.

I believe a major challenge nationwide that hinders the promotion of African American writers and other diverse writers in libraries is that there is little or no committed budget to finance these programs. Committed programming budgets are needed to establish the promotion of African American writers as part of cultural educational programming initiatives in libraries of all types. During my career, monies for promotion of events involving African American writers through library programming often involved a great deal of persuasion of library administrators to provide the funds to support them, and this was an issue that other colleagues had in common with me over the years. Programmers employed in libraries or other organizations of a similar type should have a solid budget line to use to meet programming needs.

I recommend that library programmers with innovative ideas that feature African American authors or other programming ventures continue to be initiators of project ideas. Build or join existing partnerships to support the ideas of others, while at the same time, be an advocate for your own programs. Learn to be a good negotiator for more quid pro quo in relationships. Learn to be a strong and savvy negotiator.

As a full disclosure, in writing this autoethnographic text and guidebook on programming to promote African American writers it was only fair that I disclose my sociocultural background. The field of ethnography establishes that how we perceive the world and how we act stem in part from our cultural background. I am an African American female who grew up and worked in midwestern small to mid-sized cities all my life. My whole professional career has been spent working in libraries: one public library and several academic libraries. All the academic institutions where I've worked had predominately White teaching faculty and White student body enrollments, sometimes referred to as predominantly White institutions (PWIs).

My sociocultural background and experience affect how I see and navigate the world. For example, if I'd worked at a historically Black college or university (HBCU) or lived and worked in a place with a larger African

American population or other populations of People of Color, undoubtedly my experiences and my outlooks would be different. As an African American I've lived and worked as a minority in small to mid-sized midwestern cities all my life. I've personally always focused on working collaboratively with persons of all races, ethnicities, and socioeconomic and cultural backgrounds.

As I stated at the introduction of this book, I hold the position that well-designed programming centered on African American writers should be combined with effective promotion and solid partnerships. That approach, I believe, will lead to library best practice. The latter has been the principle on which I've worked over the years as an organizer and as a coordinator of library programming. In this conclusion, I will once again sum up the advantages of building partnership teams for the purpose of programming to promote African American writers.

Building partnerships for programs achieves the following broad advantages: 1) nurtures relationships and strengthens a library's organizational ties to the community; 2) shares the workload among program organizers; 3) disperses costs among willing, generous contributors; 4) demonstrates or showcases the strengths of your program team; and 5) spawns new ideas for collaboration.

Programmers who promote diversity programs can and should strive to build partnerships within institutional lines and outside of their home institutions, whenever possible, to surrounding communities. These types of partnerships are highly advantageous for a community's total development. For well over a decade, I served as chairperson of the Springfield African American Read-In (AARI), a collaborative partnership of five local institutions, which was part of a national initiative sponsored by the National Association for the Council of Teachers of English (NCTE). The Springfield AARI successfully sponsored programs, many of which are covered in this book, to accomplish our citywide twofold goal: 1) to promote African American writers, and 2) to help build a community of readers and lifelong learners.

IMPLICATIONS FOR THE FUTURE OF LIBRARIES

Libraries are changing and forming new models. One functional area for community development that libraries of all types and sizes will provide into the future is programming. Programming is a function that will help to keep libraries viable contributors to communities as social–cultural institutions in the years to come. Librarians, especially, are champions in three areas of service for library users: 1) information literacy, 2) cultural literacy, and 3) support and encouragement of reading.

Promoting African American writers through programming can contribute to improving information literacy and cultural literacy and motivate lifelong reading and learning among the citizens of communities. This is accomplished by reaching one individual at a time, teaching groups of children and youth, or by providing multiple opportunities for members of a cross-section of the community to gather and positively interact with one another and to learn from each other.

Words from a school library journal article aptly summarize the benefits of making available to students books written by diverse writers and representing the perspectives of a range of cultures in school library collections: "[I]ntegrating these materials into school curricula and into students' leisure reading habits can provide a sense of belonging among immigrant and minority youth, facilitate student learning, foster acceptance of individual differences, and increase student knowledge about the world" (Agosto, 2007, 27–28).

Individuals become culturally competent along a spectrum of growth and knowledge in three ways (Overall, 2009): (1) through their lived experience initially in the culture they are born into, then (2) by interacting and communicating with persons from other cultures, and lastly (3) by reading about the history and culture they were born into as well as learning about the histories and cultures of others. Libraries can be a central place where persons become information literate, culturally competent, and lifelong readers and learners.

BENEFITS OF WRITING THIS BOOK FOR THE AUTHOR

In the introduction, I state that the coordination and development of programming in my professional work has become one of my life's passions. Writing this book as a guide and an autoethnography has helped me to take a reflective look back on a major part of my librarian career.

Writing about my experiences has been an illuminating self-reflection in many ways. It has allowed me to see, in hindsight, some things that I did not see when I was traveling along my career path or actively presenting programs. Writing this book has allowed me to see the beauty of the library programs created around African American writers. I see more clearly the substantial accomplishments in my library career and some of the hurdles that I've overcome, as well as some mistakes I've made. I can relate to what one autoethnography researcher had to say about the process:

> Doing autoethnography involves a back-and-forth movement between experiencing and examining a vulnerable self and observing and revealing the broader context of that experience. (Ellis, 2007, 14)

It's important to prepare the next generation to lead, and it's my hope that by writing this book I have made a step in the right direction of helping others to take the lead to promote African American writers and African American literature through library programming.

A THANK-YOU TO CASE CONTRIBUTORS

I want to thank all those who wrote case example contributions to this book. I appreciate those librarians and others who took the time to respond to my call for case examples of programs that promote African American authors that involved partnerships. The contributing writers shared case examples of programs that made or that are making a positive difference in their communities. I am forever grateful to those who showed the willingness to share! Their work demonstrated programming skill, innovation, and creativity. In reading their case examples, I thought of two common characteristics of strong library programmers. One is a continuous striving to please public program audiences by striving to meet their wants and needs. Second, programmers are constantly recruiting staff members and/or volunteers who possess an array of talents to assist in the responsibilities of making programs happen. I hope that this book can help those within the librarianship profession to address the challenges associated with programming, as well as gain a greater appreciation among others of programs' benefits. This book is filled with practical tips on how to satisfy audiences and how to work effectively together with program partners and volunteers.

REFERENCES

Agosto, Denise E. "Building a Multicultural School Library: Issues and Challenges." *Teacher Education* 34, no. 3 (2007): 27–31.

Cruz, Alice M. "Intentional Integration of Diversity Ideals in Academic Libraries: A Literature Review." *Journal of Academic Librarianship* 45 (2019): 220–227.

Ellis, Carolyn. "Telling Secrets, Revealing Lives: Relational Ethics in Research with Intimate Others." *Qualitative Inquiry* 13, no. 1 (2007): 3–29.

Overall, Patricia Montiel. "Cultural Competence: A Conceptual Framework for Library and Information Science Professionals." *Library Quarterly* 79, no. 2 (2009): 175–204.

Appendix

BRIEF BIOGRAPHIES OF AFRICAN AMERICAN WRITERS AND CULTURE KEEPERS

Brief biographical notes are provided here for suggested writers and culture keepers to feature in programs whose names are listed in Chapter 1. Biographical information was found using the databases *Oxford African American Studies Center*, the *Biographical Reference Bank*, and other online reference sources. In a few biographies, full birth date information was not found.

Abbott, Robert (November 28, 1868–February 29, 1940). Journalist and publisher. Abbot was a newspaper publisher, editor, and lawyer. In 1905, he founded the *Chicago Defender*, which became the most influential African American newspaper of the first half of the twentieth century. Born to parents who had been slaves, Abbot became a self-made millionaire. He studied printing at Hampton Institute (now Hampton University) and, in 1898, earned a law degree from Kent College of Law in Chicago (now, Chicago-Kent College of Law at the Illinois Institute of Technology).

Alexander, Kwame (August 21, 1968–). Poet and children's & young adult fiction writer. Alexander was born in Manhattan, New York. His father was a writer, and his mother was an English teacher. In his early writing career, Alexander wrote mainly poetry. In 2015, his career took off when he won both the John Newbery Medal and the Coretta Scott King Honor Award for *The Crossover* (2014), a young adult novel written in verse about boys and basketball. He wrote a sequel titled *Rebound* (2018). He followed these titles with other books written for young adults and children. Alexander studied English at Virginia Tech University and was influenced by poet Nikki Giovanni while studying there.

Angelou, Maya (April 4, 1928–May 28, 2014). Poet and memoirist. Angelou was a "Phenomenal Woman," which is the title of one of her most widely recognized poems in addition to the poem "Still I Rise." A gifted poet, autobiographer, and essayist, she wrote the first of her seven autobiographies, *I Know Why the Caged Bird Sings*, in 1969. At the time that Angelou began writing her series of autobiographies or memoirs, it was considered a unique style. *I Know Why the Caged Bird Sings* was nominated for a National Book Award.

Ashford & Simpson, Husband-and-wife songwriting and production team; Nickolas Ashford (May 4, 1941–August 22, 2011) & Valerie Simpson (August 26, 1946–). Beginning in the mid-1960s, the couple wrote R&B and pop songs that became hits for numerous recording artists. They wrote for Motown Records beginning in 1966. Ashford & Simpson were inducted into the Songwriters Hall of Fame in 2002. They were recipients of the Rhythm and Blues Foundation's Pioneer Award in 1999 and received the American Society of Composers, Authors and Publishers' (ASCAP) highest honor—the Founders Award—in 1996. The duo also had a successful singing and recording career of their own.

Baker, Augusta (April 1, 1911–February 23, 1998). Storyteller. Baker was a gifted storyteller. She served as a children's librarian for the New York Public Library, 135th Street (Countee Cullen Regional) branch in Harlem. In 1946, Baker published an extensive bibliography of titles related to the African American experience titled "Books about Negro Life for Children" (published in subsequent editions as *The Black Experience in Children's Books*). In 1977, Baker, with coauthor Ellin Greene, wrote and published the book *Storytelling: Art and Technique*.

Baldwin, James (August 2, 1924–December 1, 1987). Novelist, essayist, and playwright. Baldwin was an extraordinarily gifted and versatile writer who engaged readers with themes such as the psychology of racism, sexual identity, and America's paradoxes. His works include the novels *Go Tell It on the Mountain* (1952) and *Another Country* (1964); books of essays *Notes of a Native Son* (1956), *Nobody Knows My Name* (1961), and *The Fire Next Time* (1963); and plays *The Amen Corner* (1955) and *Blues for Mister Charlie* (1964).

Brown, Echo (birthdate unavailable). Author and storyteller. Brown is from Cleveland, Ohio. An alumna of Dartmouth, she was the first person in her family to graduate from college. Brown is the author of the award-winning book *Black Girls Unlimited: The Remarkable Story of a Teenage Wizard* (2020). She wrote and starred in a one-woman show titled "Black Virgins Are Not Hipsters," which toured for two years in cities in the United States and Europe. She is described as a "visionary storyteller who creates and performs inspiring one woman shows" by the goodreads website.

Bryan, Ashley (July 13, 1923–February 4, 2022). Storyteller and children's book author. Bryan was born in the Bronx, New York. He attended the Cooper Union School of Art and Engineering before being drafted into the U.S. Army at age nineteen. He served in WWII and continued his love of drawing. After the war, he completed his degree at Cooper Union and using the GI Bill studied philosophy and literature at Columbia University. He won a Fulbright Scholarship and went to Europe to study art. One of his greatest accomplishments was to paint a portrait of renowned cellist Pablo Casals in

Paris, France. When Bryan returned to the United States, he became a successful children's book author, illustrator, and storyteller. One of his most successful children's books was *Beautiful Blackbird*, which won the Coretta Scott King Book Award in 2003. Bryan refined his storytelling through the telling of traditional African tales and stories based on African American spirituals. His storytelling combined singing, movement, and puppets. Bryan was awarded the Coretta Scott King-Virginia Hamilton Lifetime Achievement Award, Laura Ingalls Wilder Medal, and the New York Public Library's Literary Lions Award, among others.

Bullins, Ed (July 2, 1935–November 13, 2021). Playwright. Bullins was born in Philadelphia. He dropped out of high school and served in the U.S. Navy (1952–1955). Bullins resumed his education and completed a BA degree from Antioch University in Yellow Springs, Ohio, and an MFA degree from San Francisco State College. Bullins was a leader in the Black Arts Movement of the late 1960s and 1970s and helped to create Black Theater during the Black Arts Movement, which promoted Black nationalism. Bullins moved to New York City in the 1960s, where he produced in 1968 his first full-length play, *In the Wine Time*. The play examined the lack of opportunities available to the urban poor and was the first of a series of plays called the Twentieth Century Cycle. Bullins wrote scores of plays during his career that spanned decades. In addition, he wrote essays, short stories, and poetry. He won three Obie Awards and was awarded two Guggenheim grants. In 1995, he became a professor of theater at Northeastern University in Boston, where he taught until his death.

Butler, Octavia (June 22, 1947–February 24, 2006). Science fiction writer. Butler was recipient of numerous awards for her writing, including multiple Hugo and Nebula awards. She was the first science fiction writer to win the prestigious MacArthur Fellowship in 1995. In 2000, Butler received the PEN American Center Lifetime Achievement Award. One of her most widely read works is the novel *Kindred* (1979).

Caines-Coggswell, Gladys (1942–). Storyteller. Caines-Coggswell was named a Master Folk Artist of Missouri in storytelling nine times. She holds a bachelor's degree in psychology and a master's degree in education, both from Washington University in St. Louis, Missouri. Learning storytelling from her great grandmother, Caines-Coggswell participated in storytelling competitions nationally and internationally with meritorious placing in many. She is the author of *Stories from the Heart: Missouri African American Heritage* (2009), for which she received the Distinguished Literary Achievement Award from the Governor's Humanities Council.

Campbell, Bill (birthdate unavailable). Graphic novelist. Campbell's early solo works include *Sunshine Patriots* (published 2004, originally written in 1998). In 2013, he coedited with Edward Austin Hall the groundbreaking anthology *Mothership: Tales from Afrofuturism and Beyond*. In 2021, Campbell won a Locus Award for his work helping to diversify the field of science fiction.

Coates, Ta-Nehisi (September 30, 1975–). Journalist, memoirist, and novelist. An award-winning journalist who writes for *Atlantic Magazine*, Coates's landmark article on reparations, originally published in the *Atlantic*, was reprinted in a collection of essays he edited about the Obama presidency, *We Were Eight Years in Power* (2018). Coates was born and grew up in Baltimore, Maryland. His parents founded Black Classic Press. Coates has written three memoirs, one of which, *Between the World and Me* (2015), won the National Book Award. His debut novel, *The Water Dancer* (2020), is a fantasy and received critical acclaim.

Cleveland, James (December 5, 1931–February 9, 1991). Singer and songwriter, gospel composer. Cleveland wrote more than four hundred gospel songs, as well as composed and arranged gospel music. The lead singer of a group called the James Cleveland Singers, he also had a solo singing career. Cleveland founded the Gospel Music Workshop of America. He sold millions of records and won three Grammy Awards. He mentored rhythm & blues singer Aretha Franklin, from a child to adulthood; pop music artist Billy Preston; and other musical artists. He was the first gospel artist to have a star on the Hollywood Walk of Fame.

Cullen, Countee (May 30, 1903–January 9, 1946). Poet and dramatist. Cullen was born Countee LeRoy Porter, but there is little documentation of his early childhood. He was twice adopted by his paternal grandmother, whom he lived with in New York from ages nine to eleven. Cullen was then adopted by Frederick Ashbury Cullen, a minister at the Salem Methodist Church in Harlem. Cullen began writing poetry as a youngster, and his first poem, "To the Swimmer," was published in the magazine *The Modern School* during his sophomore year of high school. Cullen was an excellent student and was inducted into the Arista Honor Society. During his college years, he wrote poetry that was widely published in journals such as the *Century Magazine, Harper's*, and *Poetry*. Cullen graduated from New York University in 1925 with a bachelor's degree. He received a master's degree from Harvard University in 1926. Cullen received a Guggenheim Award, which allowed him a year of study in Paris. He published a collection of his poetry, *Copper Sun*, and a work titled *The Ballad of the Brown Girl*; and edited the anthology *Caroling Dusk: An Anthology of Verse by Negro Poets*, all in 1927. He continued publishing widely with several other poetry collections, the novel *One Way to Heaven* (1932), various children's books, and several plays including *St. Louis Woman* (1945) with Arna Bontemps (off Broadway). His final collection of poems was published posthumously titled *On These I Stand* (1947), which contains eighty-nine poems.

Dash, Julie (October 22, 1952–). Screenwriter and film director. Dash was the first African American female to direct a feature-length film. The film, *Daughters of the Dust* (1982), is based on the unique African American Gullah culture found in South Carolina's Sea Islands. Dash's father grew up on the Sea Islands before migrating to New York. *Daughters of the Dust* is a unique, documentary-quality film deemed a national treasure by the Library of Congress. Dash earned a bachelor's degree in film production from City College of New York before moving to Los Angeles to develop her filmmaking skills. She earned an MFA in motion picture and television from the University of California, Los Angeles.

Davis, Angela (January 26, 1944–). Nonfiction writer, political activist, and philosopher. Born in Birmingham, Alabama. Davis's parents were both teachers. She graduated from Brandeis University in 1965 with degrees in philosophy and French literature. She began her doctoral studies in Germany but returned home after learning of the political unrests in the United States. Davis enrolled at the University of California-San Diego to finish her doctoral studies. She became a member of the Black Panther Party (BPP), the Student Non-Violent Coordinating Committee (SNCC), and the Communist Party. She was involved in prison reform and was an advocate for African American political prisoners. When an attempted prison escape turned deadly in a California courtroom, Davis was arrested and jailed as an accomplice but was later acquitted. She has written extensively on race, class, gender, and the criminal justice system. Her trailblazing book *Women, Race, and Class* was published in 1981. She published the book *Are Prisons Obsolete?* in 2003, and a compilation of her writing on critical race feminism was published in 1998.

Dorsey, Thomas (July 1, 1899–January 23, 1993). Gospel songwriter, pianist, and composer. Dorsey contributed to the formal development of American gospel music as both a songwriter and composer. Born in Villa Rica, Georgia, he was the son of an African American preacher, but he moved to Atlanta at age eleven where he was influenced by local blues piano. During WWI, Dorsey moved to Chicago and studied at the Chicago College of Composition and Arranging. He worked as an agent for Paramount Records. He composed and played piano for talented blues singers and jazz musicians and later formed his own jazz band in which Ma Rainey performed. Dorsey's first written gospel song, "Someday, Somewhere," was published in the collection *Gospel Pearls* (1921). In the 1930s, he turned his songwriting and composing completely to gospel music. In 1932, he opened the first publishing house for African American gospel music, the Thomas A. Dorsey Gospel Songs Music Publishing Company. Dorsey's influence on gospel songwriting was pivotal. He wrote many classic gospel songs, including "Precious Lord, Take My Hand" (1932), which he composed after his wife's death.

Douglass, Frederick (February 14, 1817–February 20, 1895). Journalist and writer. Born in Tuckahoe, Maryland, to an enslaved mother of African American heritage and an unknown White father, Douglass escaped slavery and went to New York, where he later married a free colored woman, Anna Murray. He joined the Massachusetts Anti-Slavery Society and traveled for the society, giving abolitionist speeches. In 1845, he wrote an autobiography, *Narrative of the Life of Frederick Douglass, an American Slave, Written by Himself.* He wrote a second autobiography, *My Bondage and My Freedom,* in 1855. Douglass started a newspaper, the *North Star* (later called *Frederick Douglass's Paper*). He wrote many of the articles for and published his newspaper from 1847 until 1860. Douglass was active before, during, and after the civil war, providing leadership as an orator and writer.

Dove, Rita (August 28, 1952–). Poet. Dove published many books of poetry, a book of short stories, a novel, and a play. She was awarded the Pulitzer Prize for Poetry in 1987 for *Thomas and Beulah,* about her maternal grandparents who migrated North from the oppression of the South. Dove's poems examine the lives of ordinary people and their experiences with injustices of racism, sexism, and classism. Dove, as a child, knew of the painful experience of racism through her father, who was hired as an elevator operator although he had earned a graduate degree in chemistry from University of Akron and was denied employment in that field at Goodyear Tire in Akron, Ohio because of employment discrimination. One of his former professors intervened, and her father was eventually hired as the first African American chemist at the Goodyear Tire plant. Dove was the youngest poet laureate of the United States (1993–1995). Her achievements include being named a Mellon Fellow by the National Humanities Center (1988–1989), named Phi Beta Kappa poet by Harvard University (1993), and being given NAACP's Great American Artist Award (1993). Dove became the Commonwealth Professor of English at the University of Virginia in 1993.

Dr. Dre (February 18, 1965–). Hip-hop artist/writer and record executive. Born André Romelle Young in Los Angeles to parents who were semiprofessional musicians. Young's nickname, Dr. Dre, came from an admiration of basket player Julius "Dr. J" Erving. It was due to Young's early passion as a teenager with music that he became talented in the use of electronic equipment and performing as a disc jockey. Young became a leader in the development of hip-hop with his role in the groups World Class Wreckin' Cru and N.W.A. (Niggaz with Attitude), which released the controversial single "Fuck the Police"; and as a solo artist with his debut, Grammy Award-winning album, *The Chronic*. In 1996, Young founded his own production company, Aftermath Records, which brought him continued success. His production company signed on new hip-hop talent Marshall "Eminem" Mathers. In 2000, Young won a Grammy Award for Producer of the Year.

Drury, Jackie Sibblies (1982–). Playwright. Drury won a Pulitzer Prize for Drama in 2019 for *Fairview*, a play about racism in theatre. Drury mixes humor into her playwrighting on deeply serious topics, a trait that stems from her admiration of comedian Richard Pryor. The Pulitzer Committee said her award-winning play "ultimately bring[s] audiences into the actors' community to face deep-seated prejudices." Earlier in her career she won the 2010 Ignition Festival of New Plays Award for a play about African American actors in a play depicting genocide of the Herero tribe in Namibia by Germans. Drury was born in Plainfield, New Jersey, and raised in the town by her mother and paternal grandmother, both Jamaican immigrants. She earned her BA in theatre from Yale University and MFA from Brown University.

DuVernay, Ava (August 24, 1972–). Screenwriter and producer. DuVernay is the first African American woman to earn a Sundance Film Festival Award, in 2012, for directing *Middle of Nowhere*, which follows a woman whose husband receives an eight-year prison sentence. She is the first African American woman to be nominated for a Golden Globe Award for best director, for *Selma* (2014), about the fight for voting rights in Alabama. DuVernay, along with codirector and co-screenwriter Spencer Averick, was nominated for the 2017 Academy Award for best documentary feature for *13th*, about mass incarceration of African American men. DuVernay has received awards and nominations for directing and screenwriting from the African American film industry and others, including the Hollywood Black Film Festival, Black Reel Awards, African American Film Critics Association, and the NAACP Image Awards for Outstanding Independent Motion Picture. DuVernay holds a BA degree in English and African American Studies from University of California, Los Angeles.

Dyson, Michael Eric (October 23, 1958–). Writer and clergyman. Dyson writes about African American culture and politics in a way that is understandable to both the layperson and academics. Born and raised in the ghettos of Detroit, Michigan, he was an avid reader and good student. Heavily influenced by the Black church, he became an ordained minister in 1981. He earned a BA at Carson-Newman College in 1982, and an MA and PhD at Princeton University in 1991 and 1993. Dyson has taught at several major universities, and currently is a professor in the Divinity School at Vanderbilt University. He has written more than twenty books on a everything from music and religion (*Between God and Gangsta Rap: Bearing Witness to Black Culture*, 1996), to Katrina (*Come Hell or High Water: Hurricane Katrina and the Color of Disaster*, 2006), to the meaning of the Obama presidency (*The Black Presidency: Barack Obama and the Politics of Race in America*, 2016).

Ewing, Eve L. (1986–) Poet. Ewing published, in 2017, a collection of poetry entitled *Electric Arches* with poems and art about growing up in Chicago. *Electric Arches* won numerous best poetry awards, including the Norma Farber Award for first book of poetry from the Poetry Society of America. Ewing is the author of the *Ironheart* comic book, published by Marvel, that centers on heroine Riri Williams. She is an education scholar with a BA in English language and literature from University of Chicago, an MEd from Dominican University, and an MA in educational policy and management from Harvard University. She earned a PhD in education from Harvard (2018) and wrote her dissertation on Chicago school closings. Ewing taught in Chicago public schools from 2008 to 2011. She is an assistant professor at the School of Social Service Administration at University of Chicago.

Flowers, Ebony (birthdate unavailable) Cartoonist and ethnographer. Flower published her graphic novel *Hot Combs* in 2019 to high critical praise and has received many awards including the 2020 Eisner for Best Short Story and the 2020 Ignatz for Outstanding Graphic Novel. Flowers holds a BA in biological anthropology from University of Maryland College Park and a PhD in curriculum and instruction from the University of Wisconsin-Madison.

Gates, Henry Louis, Jr. (September 16, 1950–). Writer. Gates is a prolific writer and editor of African American history and literature. He was born to working-class parents in Keyser, West Virginia. Gates was a committed student and was awarded an Andrew W. Mellon scholarship to study at Yale University. He graduated from Yale with a degree in history. Gates won a Ford Foundation Fellowship to study for a doctorate at Cambridge University. There he met and studied under Nigerian writer Wole Soyinka, who influenced him to change his research interest to literature. Gates developed a literary theory called "the Black idiom," which on the one hand was a groundbreaking feat, but on the other hand received strong criticisms. He became a professor at Harvard University in 1991. Gates is responsible for recovering African American literature and popularizing it into edited reference volumes that include the *Schomburg Library of Nineteenth Century Black Women Writers* (1991) and *The Oxford Companion to African American Literature*, coedited with William L. Andrews et al. (1997).

Hamilton, Virginia (March 12, 1934–February 19, 2002). Children's author. Hamilton decided she wanted to write children's books early in her life and she became a prolific writer. She learned the craft of storytelling growing up with family members who were storytellers like her maternal grandfather, who had escaped slavery by crossing the Ohio River. Hamilton studied literature and creative writing at Antioch College on a full scholarship for three years before she transferred to the Ohio State University for one year. She then studied at the New School for Social Research in New York. Hamilton wrote in a variety of genres and in her long career was successful in publishing nearly one book each year. Her most well-known book, *M. C. Higgins, the Great* (1974), was the first book by an African American author to win the prestigious John Newbery Medal. Over the years, Hamilton won nearly every major award offered in children's literature.

Hansberry, Lorraine (May 19, 1930–January 12, 1965). Playwright. Hansberry was born and raised into a middle-class African American family in Chicago. She wrote her classic play *Raisin in the Sun* in 1954. The play won the New York Drama Critics Award. Hansberry was the first African American woman to have a play performed on Broadway when *Raisin in the Sun* opened there in 1959 and ran for nineteen months. The play's storyline follows the struggles of an African American family to buy a "dream house" in an area that discriminates against non-White homeownership. Furthermore, the play examines the inner dynamics and conflicts of an extended, working-class African American family. Hansberry died from illness at age thirty-five. A play using excerpts of her work was written posthumously about Hansberry titled *To Be Young, Gifted, and Black* by her husband, Robert Nemiroff.

Hill, Lauryn (May 26, 1975). Hip-hop writer and spoken word artist. Born in South Orange, New Jersey, Hill gained early success as a singer and actor as a teenager in the soap opera *As the World Turns* and in the movie *Sister Act 2: Back in the Habit* (1993). At the same time, 1993, Hill met Haitian immigrants Wyclef Jean and Prakazrel "Pras" Michel, and the three formed the hip-hop group Fugees (short for Refugees). Their first album was unsuccessful, but the second, *The Score* (1996), sold more than seventeen million copies as the result of a marketing tour. In 1998, Hill released her debut solo album, *The Miseducation of Lauryn Hill*, which she wrote and produced. A mixture of hip-hop, reggae, gospel, and soul music, it became an astronomical success. Hill was nominated for ten Grammy Awards and won five (the most for a woman). She won the Album of the Year, which was the first time that had been achieved by a hip-hop album. Unfortunately, Hill's second album was a disappointment, and she was not able to regain the level of success she had achieved prior.

Holland-Dozier-Holland: Brian Holland (February 15, 1941–), Lamont Dozier (June 16, 1941–), and Eddie Holland (October 30, 1939–). Songwriting and music production team. Brian and Eddie Holland are brothers. Lamont Dozier is their friend and collaborator. All grew up in Detroit, Michigan. The trio have had a long and productive music career working together. Dozier and Eddie Holland pursued careers as singers prior to their collaboration with Brian Holland. In 1963, Berry Gordy signed the trio to work for Motown. Holland-Dozier-Holland are responsible for helping to create the Motown sound through songwriting and production work they performed for many of the Motown artists, including Martha and the Vandellas, the Four Tops, Marvin Gaye, and the Supremes. Holland-Dozier-Holland were inducted into the Rock and Roll Hall of Fame in 1990 for their songwriting and record production. A memoir, *Come and Get These Memories*, written by Brian and Eddie Holland with Dave Thompson, was published in 2019.

Hunter-Gault, Charlayne (February 27, 1942–). Journalist. Hunter-Gault was a trailblazer in American print and broadcast journalism. The first African American writer for the *Louisville Times* and *The New Yorker*, she later worked as a correspondent, beginning in the 1990s, for *The MacNeil/Lehrer Report* (later named the PBS *News Hour*). As a college student, Hunter-Gault was one of the first African American students to integrate the University of Georgia and throughout her career has provided commentary on civil rights issues and interviewed civil and human rights leaders including Nelson Mandela.

Hurston, Zora Neale (January 7, 1891–January 28, 1960). Novelist, folklorist, and storyteller. Hurston was born in Notasulga, Alabama. When she was a child, Hurston's family moved to Eatonville, Florida, which was the first all-Black incorporated town in the country. At age thirteen, Hurston's mother died. At age sixteen, she moved to New York. She wrote during the Harlem Renaissance period and was part of a circle of successful African American writers, including Langston Hughes, with whom she wrote a play, *Mule Bone*. She became a pioneer writer of folk fiction. She wrote about African American life in the South. Hurston's writing was influenced by her studies of anthropology under Franz Boas at Barnard College. She studied at Howard University for a few years (1921–1924) before winning a scholarship to study at Barnard. She graduated from the school in 1928. She was the recipient in 1925 of a Guggenheim Award and traveled to Europe to study. Hurston's published works include *Mules and Men* (1935), *Their Eyes Were Watching God* (1937), and *Tell My Horse* (1938). She died in 1960 at age sixty-two in destitution. Her work was rediscovered in the 1980s, and since that time several of her works-in-progress were published posthumously.

Jemisin, N. K. (September 19, 1972–). Science fiction and fantasy writer. Jemisin is the first writer to receive the prestigious Hugo Award for best novel in science fiction or fantasy for three consecutive years, The Broken Earth Trilogy: *The Stone Sky* (2017), *The Obelisk Gate* (2016), and *The Fifth Season* (2015). Nora Keita Jemisin was born in Iowa City, Iowa, grew up in Mobile, Alabama, and spent summers with her father in New York City. She publishes using her first and middle initials and her surname. Jemison earned a bachelor of science degree in psychology from Tulane University in New Orleans and an MEd at University of Maryland at College Park. While in college, Jemisin began writing science fiction in her free time. In her first attempt to get published she sent out two completed science fiction novels and received rejection letters for them both. She then turned to a writers' workshop to get help on writing, and one of the recommendations she received was to begin by writing short stories. One of her early published short stories, "Non-Zero Probabilities" (2009), was a nominee for both the Hugo and Nebula awards. She later included this short story in a collection of short stories about Afrofuturism, *How Long 'til Black Future Month?* (2013), which won the Locus Award for science fiction, and was nominated for both British Fantasy and World Fantasy awards. Jemisin continued to write short story science fiction and fantasy as well as novels, quickly publishing more than seven science fiction and fantasy novels, most receiving prestigious awards or nominations. She received a MacArthur Fellowship in 2020 and a Karl Edgar Wagner Award in 2018.

Johnson, John H. (January 19, 1918–August 6, 2005). Publisher and journalist. Johnson was born in Arkansas City, Arkansas. As a teenager, he moved with his family to Chicago, where he graduated from Du Sable High School. He attended University of Chicago. As a college student, Johnson worked for the Supreme Life Insurance Company, where he was given the job of compiling weekly newspaper clippings to keep his boss current on news events. This gave Johnson the idea to start a magazine, the *Negro Digest*, which he began publishing in 1942. The title of the *Negro Digest* was later changed to *Black World*. In 1951, Johnson launched *Ebony*, an African American news magazine. He also began *Jet*, the world's largest-circulations African American news weekly. His business enterprises expanded to book publishing and later to the Fashion Fair Cosmetics Company. Johnson received numerous awards, including the NAACP Spingarn Medal, the Most Outstanding Black Publisher in History Award from the National Newspapers Association, and the Presidential Medal of Freedom from President Bill Clinton.

Kendi, Ibram X (August 13, 1982–). Writer. Kendi became the founding director of the Boston University Center for Antiracist Research in 2020. He published his book *How to Be an Antiracist* in 2019, which was a *New York Times* bestseller and won the National Book Award. Kendi published *Stamped from the Beginning: The Definitive History of Racist Ideas in America* (2016) that also won the National Book Award and made him the youngest recipient of the award. In 2022, he coedited with Keisha N. Blain an anthology of nonfiction and fiction, *Four Hundred Souls: A Community History of African America 1619–2019*, that received critical acclaim and became a *New York Times* bestseller. Kendi's first book, *The Black Campus Movement* (2012), won the W. E. B. Du Bois Prize. Kendi has published numerous scholarly articles in academic journals, as well as many op-ed pieces in newspapers and magazines. He received a BA in journalism from the University of Florida and a PhD from Temple University in African American Studies. He has taught at SUNY Oneonta, SUNY Albany, the University of

Florida, and American University. In 2017, Kendi became a full professor with an endowed professorship at Boston University. In 2019, he was awarded the prestigious Guggenheim Fellowship.

King, Martin Luther, Jr. (January 15, 1929–April 4, 1968). Minister and civil rights leader. King led a nonviolent civil disobedience Civil Right Movement in the United States patterned after that of Mahatma Gandhi, leader of the India Civil Rights Movement in India. King motivated followers with his speeches, which called persons into action, to march for civil rights and protest injustices using nonviolent tactics for change, although they were often met by violent retaliation and jail sentences. Major stands led by King include the 1956 Montgomery, Alabama Bus Boycott for the integration of public buses, the 1963 March on Washington, D.C. for Jobs and Freedom, and the 1965 Voter Registration Drive in Selma, Alabama. King was assassinated in 1968 in Memphis, Tennessee, while organizing in support of the rights of sanitation workers. Born in Atlanta, Georgia, he was the son of a prominent minister and pastor of the Ebenezer Baptist Church in Atlanta. King received a bachelor's in divinity degree from Crozier Seminary in 1951. On June 18, 1953, he married Coretta Scott, with whom he had four children. King published his first book in 1958, *Stride Toward Freedom: The Montgomery Story*, a memoir about the Montgomery boycott and an articulation of his view on the application of the philosophies of Gandhi and Reinhold Niebuhr. King is also known for his writing from a jail cell his 1963 "Letter from a Birmingham Jail," in which he addressed, particularly to clergy, the moral responsibility to break unjust laws through nonviolent, direct action. On August 28, 1963, King delivered his famous "I Have a Dream" speech that led to President Lyndon Johnson's signing of the Voting Rights Act of 1965.

Lamar, Kendrick (June 17, 1987–). Also known as Kendrick Lamar Duckworth. Writer/rapper. In the late 1980s, Lamar's parents moved from Chicago to Compton, where he was born. Competitive at an early age, Lamar learned by first listening to the rap music of others. In 2009, he released a digital-only mixed tape, *Overly Dedicated*, also known as *O(verly) D(edicated)* or O.D., which appeared on the Billboard R&B/Hip-hop chart in 2010. He worked hard to produce his first major-label album in 2012, *Good Kid, M.A.A.D. City*. The album sold 242,122 copies during its first week. Lamar received six Grammy Award nominations in 2015 and won five awards, including best rap performance and best rap song for "Alright," best rap/sung collaboration for "These Walls," and best rap album for *To Pimp a Butterfly*. He won a 2018 Pulitzer Prize for Music for his album *Damn* (2017), which won the 2018 Grammy Award for best rap album. Lamar is credited for many of the soundtrack songs in the Marvel comic turned into hit box-office movie *Black Panther*.

Lee, Spike (March 20, 1957–). Screenwriter and filmmaker. Spike Lee was born with the given name Shelton Jackson, the eldest of five children, to middle-class parents in Atlanta, Georgia. His father was a jazz musician, and his mother was a schoolteacher. At a young age, Spike Lee's family moved to the Brooklyn borough of New York, where he spent his formative years. Lee, like his father and grandfather, attended Morehouse University, where he graduated with a bachelor's degree in communications. He went on to study at New York University, Graduate Film School. The first films that he produced were about college life loosely based on his time at Morehouse. Lee wrote, produced, edited, and acted in his debut film, *She's Gotta Have It* (1986). He went on to have a career spanning more than three decades in which he produced more than thirty-five films. Many of his films center on social and political issues in the African American experience, including *Do the Right Thing* (1989). He won an Academy Award for Best Adapted Screenplay for the film *Blackkklansman* (2016). He won both Emmy and Peabody awards for his television documentary about the hurricane Katrina aftermath, *When the Levees Broke: A Requiem in Four Acts*, 2006 and 2007 respectively.

Malcolm X (February 19, 1925–February 21, 1965). Orator and civil rights leader. The name Malcolm X was taken after Malcom Little joined the Nation of Islam, which proclaimed that his surname "Little," like other surnames used by Blacks in America, was a slave name. Malcolm X became a strong spokesperson in public rallies and speeches for Black nationalism and the ideologies of the Nation of Islam that viewed Whites as "devils." When Malcolm X discovered that Elijah Muhammad, leader of the Nation of Islam, had violated some strict moral codes, he disavowed the leader and went on a religious pilgrimage or mecca in Africa. During the mecca, he was met with warmth and brotherhood by persons of all colors who practiced Islam, which caused him to reevaluate how Islam was being practiced in the United States. Malcolm X changed his name to El-Shabazz. When he returned to the United States, he began to revise some of his views and criticisms against the nonviolence, civil disobedience philosophy of civil rights leader Martin Luther King Jr. However, El-Shabazz was soon assassinated before he could fully reframe his own new ideas. The extraordinary life story of El-Shabazz was recounted to writer Alex Haley, who wrote and published it as *The Autobiography of Malcolm X* (1965).

Marshall, Nate (1989–). Poet. Marshall wrote a collection of poems titled *Finna* in 2020 that was recognized by NPR and the New York Public Library as one of the best books of poetry of the year. His book *Wild Hundreds* (2015) won the Agnes Lynch Starrett Prize, the Black Caucus of the American Library Association Award for Poetry Book of the Year, and the Great Lakes College Association's New Writers Award. Marshall served as a coeditor of *The BreakBeat Poets: New American Poetry in the Hip-Hop Age* (2015). His poetry has appeared in *Poetry, Indiana Review, The New Republic,* and other journals. Marshall was raised in the West Pullman neighborhood of Chicago. He completed an MFA in creative writing at the University of Michigan's Helen Zell Writers Program and holds a BA in English and African American diaspora studies from Vanderbilt University.

Morrison, Toni (February 18, 1931–August 5, 2019). Novelist and essayist. With the given name of Chloe Anthony Wofford. Morrison was the second of four children born to parents who lived and raised their family in the steel town of Lorain, Ohio. She graduated with honors from high school and went on to study at Howard University in Washington, D.C. After earning a bachelor's degree from Howard, she went to graduate school and studied English at Cornell University. Morrison's first novel, *The Bluest Eye*, was published in 1970 to critical praise. It was followed by *Sula* (1973) and *Song of Solomon* (1977). Her fourth novel, *Beloved* (1987), concerns a mother who commits infanticide while attempting to escape slavery. The novel won her the highest literary praise, the Nobel Prize in Literature, as well as the Pulitzer Prize. It was adapted for theatre and movie productions. Morrison won the Nobel Prize for Literature in 1993. Her ten novels paint a masterpiece in words of the African American experience and cover centuries of human tragedy, drama, and triumph. Morrison was a master of language in telling stories. In her fiction writing she used folklore and supernatural motifs. In her literary nonfiction work *Playing in the Dark* (1992), Morrison coined the term "Africanism," defined as "the denotative and connotative blackness that African peoples have come to signify, as well as the entire range of views, assumptions, readings and misreading that accompany Eurocentric learnings about these people." She received a bachelor's degree in English with a minor in classics from Howard University, and a master's degree in English from Cornell University.

Myers, Walter Dean (August 12, 1937–July 1, 2014). Children's & young adult author. Myers published more than fifty fiction and nonfiction books for young adult readers and some children's titles. The African American characters in his fiction are portrayed realistically and without stereotype while at the same time depicting hard realities. Myers was born into a large family in the small town of Martinsburg, West Virginia. At an early age, he was adopted and raised by a family in Harlem, New York. Myers's early writing influences stem from friendships and mentorships that he formed with John Killens, James Baldwin, and others in the Harlem Writers Guild. In 1968, his book *Where Does the Day Go?* won a contest sponsored by the Council on Interracial Books for Children, which led to his successful career. He won five Coretta Scott King Awards, and his 1999 book *Monster* received the Michael Printz Award.

Nottage, Lynn (November 2, 1964–). Playwright. Nottage has twice won the Pulitzer Prize for Drama, for her plays *Ruined* in 2009 and *Sweat* in 2017. Nottage grew up in Brooklyn, New York, and was the oldest of two children. Her parents, natives of the West Indies, were established professionals who introduced their children to the arts early. Nottage attended the High School of Music and Art, located in the Harlem section of Manhattan. She attended Brown University, where she received a BA in English and creative writing. She earned an MFA from the Yale University School of Drama. In an early success, she won the 1993 Heideman Award for her play *Poof!* about an abused wife who accidently makes her abusive husband disappear. The critically acclaimed play was adapted for television on PBS and has been performed in theatres in countries worldwide. Nottage received numerous playwrighting awards over her career and was inducted on the Playwrights' Sidewalk in front of the Lucille Lortel Theatre in 2017.

Okorafor, Nnedi (April 8, 1974–). Science fiction and comics writer. Okorafor is a Nigerian American. She was born in Cincinnati, Ohio, to a Nigerian father and mother who emigrated to the United States to pursue their education. Her father became a cardiovascular surgeon, and her mother became a health administrator. As a child, Okorafor spent time in both the United States and Nigeria. She earned a BS from the University of Illinois, an MA in journalism from Michigan State University, and a doctorate in English from University of Illinois in Chicago. Okorafor writes science fiction and fantasy for both adults and children. Over the span of a decade, she wrote more than a dozen books using Nigerian myth and storytelling. Her *Akata* novel series that uses Nigerian traditional myth to tell a tale full of magic, ritual, and secrecy has been compared to J. K. Rowling's use of traditional European myth in writing the Harry Potter series. The *Akata* series centers on Sunny Nwazue, a Nigerian American girl who moves to southeastern Nigeria from New York and discovers that she belongs to the secret Leopard Society. Okorafor has won several prestigious awards for her science fiction and fantasy writing, including the Wole Soyinka Prize for Literature in Africa, the Carl Brandon Kindred Award, the World Fantasy Award for Best Novel, and the Nebula Award and Hugo Award for best novella in 2016 for the Binti trilogy. Okorafor extended her writing prowess to the realm of comic books. She wrote the digital series *Black Panther: Long Live the King.* She wrote two Marvel comic *Black Panther* series, one on Shuri, the Black Panther's sister, and another on Wakanda's female bodyguards.

Perry, Tyler (September 13, 1969–). Playwright, screenwriter, and producer. Perry was born in New Orleans, Louisiana, with the given name Emmitt Perry Jr. to parents Emmitt Perry Sr., and Willie Maxine Perry. As a child, he experienced abuse from his father and escaped from his pain by "acting out" as the class clown in school. Outside of the classroom, he found solace in reading, writing, and drawing. He dropped out of high school, changed his first name to Tyler, earned a GED or equivalent high school diploma, and became a carpenter. Perry began writing the material that would launch his theatre career when he began writing a therapeutic journal of "letters to himself," a technique he learned about through watching a television episode of *The Oprah Winfrey Show*. Initially, his staging of his debut play, *I Know I've Been Changed*, was a flop with sparse audiences that drained his savings and left him broke and homeless. He didn't give up and continued to write Christian-themed theatrical comedies. Upon moving to Atlanta, he found success by staging *I Know I've Been Changed* at the House of Blues venue. It was there that Perry connected with a famous audience member— televangelist T. J. Jakes. Tyler partnered with Jakes to create theatre productions from two of Jake's books, *Woman, Thou Art Loosed* and *Behind Closed Doors*. Perry went on to become a multimillion-dollar success, creating the outrageous grandmother character "Madea," and by playwrighting and writing screenplays for movies and for television, including some in partnership with Oprah Winfrey's TV network.

Prince, Lucy (1730–January 19, 1794). Orator and poet. Lucy Terry was stolen from her home in Africa as a small child and brought to the frontier hamlet of Deerfield, Massachusetts, where she was enslaved as the servant of Ebenezer Wells. At the age of sixteen, she wrote a poem about an Indian raid of the hamlet, "Bar's Fight," which is thought by some historians to be the first poem written by an African American. Lucy Terry married a free Black man named Abijah Prince, who bought her freedom. The couple moved to a town in Vermont. Lucy Prince spoke up for justice in her community and for her family. She gave public orations during key incidents—in a court case when she and her husband sued in a land dispute after a neighbor's fencing that they built encroached on the Princes' property, to the Governor's Council when a neighbor intentionally set fire to the Princes' property, and to college officials when her son was denied admittance to Williams College.

Queen Latifah (March 18, 1970–). Hip-hop writer/artist, singer, and actress. Born Dana Owens in Newark, New Jersey, she was nicknamed, by age eight, Queen Latifah by a cousin. Her parents separated and her mother moved Queen Latifah and her younger brother to East Newark, where they lived in the housing projects. Her mother worked two jobs while attending a community college to raise enough money to afford to move into a house. Queen Latifah started a female rap group with two friends while in high school with her mother's encouragement. The group, named Princess of the Posse, soon signed with Tommy Boy Records. The group's first album was critically acclaimed, and its second single, "Ladies First," became a rap classic and was named one of the five hundred songs "That Shaped Rock 'n' Roll" by the Rock and Roll Hall of Fame. Latifah left Tommy Records and signed with Motown, and in 1993 released her third album, *Black Reign*. In 1994, she won a Grammy Award for Best Rap Solo Performance for the album's first single, "U.N.I.T.Y." Latifah successfully pursued an acting career in television and film along with her musical career.

Reynolds, Jason (December 6, 1983–). Young adult fiction writer. Reynolds was named the National Ambassador for Young People's Literature for 2020–2021 by the Library of Congress, the Children's Book Council, and Every Child a Reader Organization after publishing more than twelve books that earned him literary accolades, as well as several awards. He writes young adult fiction with an authentic voice that speaks to many young African American males and other youth in the twenty-first century. His first novel, *When I Was the Greatest*, won the 2015 Coretta Scott King-John Steptoe Award for Young Talent. In 2016, Reynolds's second young adult novel, *As Brave as You*, won a Kirkus Prize and was chosen, in 2017, for the NAACP Image Award for Outstanding Literary Work for Youth/Teens. Reynolds won the inaugural Walter Dean Myers Award for Outstanding Children's Literature for a book he cowrote with Brendan Kiely, *All American Boys*, in 2014. He won another Myers Award in 2018 for his solo novel *Long Way Down* (2017). Reynolds was born in Washington, D.C. He graduated from University of Maryland.

Scott-Heron, Gil (April 1, 1949–May 27, 2011). Poet and singer/songwriter. Scott-Heron was born in Chicago. When his parents divorced, he went to live with his grandmother in Jackson, Tennessee. He excelled in school and was chosen to help integrate an elementary school in Jackson where he experienced brutal racism. His grandmother sent Scott-Heron back to live with his mother, who had moved to New York. He again excelled in school, learned to play the piano, and began writing mysteries. He won a scholarship to a private academy to complete his secondary education. He earned a bachelor's degree in English from Lincoln University and a master's degree in creative writing from Johns Hopkins University in Baltimore. Scott-Heron pursued a career in writing, publishing a novel, *Vulture*, and a collection of poetry, *Small Talk at 125th & Lenox*, which contained an early version of his most famous song, "The Revolution Will Not Be Televised." A talented musician and songwriter, he recorded several albums, two making the R&B charts. He was an early influencer of rap music.

Shange, Ntozake (October 18, 1948–October 27, 2018). Playwright and poet. Shange was born into an established middle-class family with the given name Paulette Williams in St. Louis, Missouri. Her father was interning to become a medical doctor when he was drafted to serve in the segregated ranks of the U.S. Air Force during the Korean War. At the time, Shange was an elementary-aged child, but she remembers having to relocate to live in segregated military bases in different cities with other African American families there. Shange earned a bachelor's degree in American Studies (1971) and a master's degree in the same subject from the University of Southern California (1973). In California, in 1973, Williams gave up her "slave name" and became Ntozake Shange; Ntozake loosely means "she who comes with her own things," and Shange refers to the gait of lions, which was the name used by her boyfriend. Shange is most widely known for her feminist play, which is written in a "choreopoem" style, *For Colored Girls Who Have Considered Suicide/When the Rainbow Is Enuf* (1976).

Shakur, Tupac (June 16, 1971–September 13, 1996). Writer/rapper. Born Lesane Parish Crooks in Brooklyn, New York. His mother, Afeni Shakur, renamed him Tupac Amaru Shakur after a Peruvian revolutionary when he was a year old. Shakur's mother was a member of the Black Panther Party, and the family moved around often. They moved across the country to Marin City, California, when Shakur was a teenager. Shakur, who used the stage name 2Pac and the alias name Makaveli, is considered one of the most influential rap songwriters of all time. His first solo album was titled *2Pacalypse Now* (1991), and his second album was released the following year, *Strictly 4 My N.I.G.G.A.Z.* Around that time, Shakur appeared in two motion pictures: *Juice*, an urban crime drama, and *Poetic Justice*, opposite Janet Jackson. He wrote songs about race in America and particularly the experiences of Black men. Much of his lyrics reflected the gang life of South Central Los Angeles that Shakur became involved in after moving to California, but there were activist rap lyrics in some of his songs as well. Shakur was convicted for a sexual assault in 1994 and served eight months in prison before being paroled. He was killed in a drive-by shooting in Las Vegas in September 1996, when he was twenty-five years old. New 2Pac albums continued to appear after Shakur's death, produced posthumously mainly from remixes of his prerecorded music. At the time of his induction into the Rock and Roll Hall of Fame in 2017, more than seventy-five million of his records had sold worldwide despite his music career spanning only five years.

Sharpton, Al (October 3, 1954–). Orator, writer, and activist. Sharpton was born with the given name Alfred Charles Sharpton Jr. in Brooklyn, New York. His father, who was an established contractor, deserted the family when his son was about ten years of age. Sharpton and an older sibling were then raised and cared for by his mother, a seamstress, while living in the housing projects and on welfare. As a child, Sharpton exhibited independence and the ability to influence others with his oratory skills. At a very early age, he began preaching at his Pentecostal Church and was called the "Boy Wonder Preacher." In 1969, at fifteen years of age, Sharpton was appointed by Rev. Jesse Jackson, civil rights leader and founder of an organization called Operation Breadbasket, to serve as youth director of the Brooklyn branch of the organization. In 1971, he resigned from Operation Breadbasket and started his own organization called the National Youth Movement. Sharpton later founded the National Action Network. His early influencers, whom he knew and interacted with personally, were former Congressman Adam Clayton Powell Jr., R&B singer James Brown, and boxing champion Muhammed Ali. Sharpton began to gain a national reputation after leading protest marches and giving speeches and oral statements on racial issues, such as against police killings of unarmed Blacks and against hate crimes by White civilians against Blacks, some that resulted in Blacks' deaths. Sharpton, for example, spoke out in marches and protested in the 2012 death of Trayvon Martin and the 2014 death of Eric Garner. His commentary was sought out by the media on a range of racial issues in the 2000s. Sharpton hosted his own syndicate talk radio show and a news commentary television show. He has written several books.

Singleton, John (January 6, 1968–April 29, 2019). Screenwriter and producer. Singleton was born and lived in South Central Los Angeles. He studied screenwriting at the University of Southern California (USC) School of Cinematic Arts. While at USC, Singleton won three writing awards. Columbia Pictures bought the script for the screenplay titled *Boyz n the Hood* that was written by Singleton for seven million dollars. Singleton produced the movie *Boyz n the Hood*, in 1991, which was nominated for an Academy Award for Best Director and for Best Original Screenplay. He followed his debut success with several other films about race relations, violence, and gang life in South Central Los Angeles that included *Poetic Justice* (1993) and *Higher Learning* (1998). The latter were box-office successes but did not receive critical acclaim. He continued his screenwriting and movie producing in the late 1990s and 2000s. His works included the 1997 historical drama *Rosewood* and the critically acclaimed *Hustle and Flow* (2005). Singleton died after suffering a stroke in 2019.

Smith, Tracey K. (April 16, 1972–). Poet. Smith served as the United States Poet Laureate from 2017 to 2019. Born in Falmouth, Massachusetts, the youngest of five children, she grew up in Northern California. Her mother was a teacher. Her father served in the U.S. Air Force and worked on the Hubble Space Telescope. Smith earned her BA degree in English, American studies, and African American studies from Harvard University. She studied creative writing and received an MFA from Columbia University. Smith wrote five collections of poetry from 2003 through 2021, winning the Pulitzer Prize for Poetry for her early collection *Life on Mars* (2011). She won several other writing awards and honors. Smith's poetry explores pop culture, race, and identity.

Stone, Chuck (July 21, 1924–April 6, 2014). Spokesperson, journalist, and writer. Charles Sumner Stone was born in St. Louis, Missouri, to solidly middle-class parents who were both employed in business. When Stone was a very young child, the family moved to Hartford, Connecticut, where he and his three sisters grew up. Stone trained with the Tuskegee airmen during WWII. After the military, he enrolled as a student at Wesleyan University, where he was the only African American student. He graduated in 1948 with a BA in political science and economics. He continued his education at the University of Chicago, where he received an MA in sociology. He then studied law for eighteen months at the University of Connecticut before joining the humanitarian CARE organization. In 1956, he was sent to the Gaza Strip and to India to distribute food. Stone married and had three children. He became heavily involved in the early Civil Rights Movement and was an outspoken advocate for it and wrote newspaper columns about its causes. He was employed as the editor for three major Black newspapers: the *New York Age* from 1958 to 1960, the *Afro-American* in Washington, D.C., from 1960 to 1963, and the *Chicago Daily Defender* from 1963 to 1964. Stone was one of only two Black news correspondents that covered the John F. Kennedy presidency and administration. From 1964 to 1967, Stone served as the chief administrative assistant to U.S. Congressional representative Adam Clayton Powell Jr. Powell was also pastor of the Abyssinian Baptist Church in Harlem. Stone was involved in the Black Power Movement and organized several national Black Power Conferences between the years of 1966 and 1968. In 1972, he became a political columnist for the *Philadelphia Daily News* and became its first Black senior editor. Stone was founding president of the National Association of Black Journalists. A leading journalist of the twentieth century, Stone wrote thousands of newspaper columns and magazine articles, as well as publishing many books. He received five honorary doctorates.

Taylor, Mildred (September 13, 1943–). Young adult novelist. Taylor won the prestigious John Newbery Medal in 1977 for *Roll of Thunder, Hear My Cry*, which was followed by the sequel, *Let the Circle Be Unbroken* (1981). Most of Taylor's six novels take place in Mississippi, the home state of her parents. Taylor's parents had migrated to Toledo, Ohio, when she was an infant. She learned about Mississippi from relatives who moved to Toledo and from many family trips as a child to visit friends and other relatives who lived in Mississippi. Taylor's father was a talented storyteller, as were other relatives. She has BA in English and an MA in journalism.

Timbaland (born Timothy Zachery Mosley, March 10, 1972–). Rapper, singer, and songwriter. Timbaland is a multitalented rapper, singer, and songwriter. In addition, he is an influential professional producer that contributed to the talent of numerous hip-hop and rhythm-and-blues artist of the twenty-first century. Born in Norfolk, Virginia, Timbaland learned how to use studio equipment under the mentorship of DeVante Swing at the age of nineteen. Timbaland worked with such artists as Missy Elliott, Magoo, and Aaliyah in her 1996 hit "One in a Million." He later worked with Jay-Z, Ginuwine, Ludacris, and Beyoncé. He began producing records for rock and pop stars such as Nelly Furtado and Justin Timberlake. Timbaland created a new record label under the umbrella of Interscope and has won several Grammy Awards.

Torrence, Jackie (February 12, 1944–November 30, 2004). Storyteller and author. Torrence was born in Chicago but grew up in the South in a farming settlement in Second Creek, North Carolina. She learned storytelling from her uncles, aunts, and grandparents. Torrence learned "Br'er Rabbit" parables that had been passed down through generations from her grandfather, Jim Carson, who had learned them from his father, who had lived as a slave. She was aware of the importance of the Br'er Rabbit tales because of their use not only to entertain and teach children but as a means of communication among enslaved peoples to plan escapes and insurrections. Torrence in her own personal life overcame many obstacles, including a speech impediment that she partly overcame and compensated for with help from teachers she encountered during her elementary and secondary schooling. Torrence was later diagnosed with a physical disability, a condition of impacted teeth that required oral surgery. She learned to excel in public speaking at an early age by writing stories that her early teachers allowed her to read in the classroom in front of her classmates and at school assemblies. Torrence attended Livingston College, where she joined the drama club. After graduating from college, she married a man she had met in college who was studying ministry. Her husband started a traveling ministry, and in her role as his spouse, Torrence continued some public speaking. The couple had a child together, but the marriage ended early in divorce. Torrence struggled to find steady employment and at one point found it in a library where she by happenchance was asked to substitute for a children's librarian to do storytelling. Torrence was an instant success, but it was a rocky start to finding her way to a lucrative career as a storyteller. She became a national and international premier storyteller and wrote three books about storytelling. Torrence died at sixty years of age from illnesses that had compounded over the years from grueling travel and periods of poverty.

Trethewey, Natasha (April 26-1966–). Poet. Trethewey was the United States Poet Laureate for two years, 2012 and 2013. Born in Gulfport, Mississippi, she received an MA in poetry from Hollis University and an MFA in poetry from the University of Massachusetts. She served as Poet Laureate of Mississippi. She has written five books of poetry. Many of her poems are about the South and its racial history. In 2007, she won the Pulitzer Prize for Poetry for her 2006 collection *Native Guard*. She published five books of poetry between 2006 and 2018.

Truth, Sojourner (1797–1883). Preacher. abolitionist, and feminist. Sojourner was born into slavery in Ulster County, New York and was called Isabella.

After she escaped to freedom, as a free woman she renamed herself Sojourner Truth. She joined the Zion National Church and became a traveling preacher. In the 1840s, Truth encountered the abolitionist and feminist views of the Northampton (Massachusetts) Association of Education and Industry, which she adopted as her own and embedded some of the ideas into her orations. Truth is often connected to an oration given at a women's rights convention held in Akron, Ohio, in 1851, in which she asked rhetorically, "Ar'n't I a woman?" Sojourner's "slave narrative," or accounting of her life during slavery, was written by Olive Gilbert. Sojourner herself published the narrative in 1850 and sold it during her speaking travels, the proceeds often being her main source of livelihood. *The Narrative of Sojourner Truth: A Bondswoman of Olden Times* was reprinted seven times.

Waithe, Lena (May 17, 1984–). Screenwriter and producer. Waithe is a writer of screenplays for television and movies. Her ambition at an early age was to become a television writer. Waithe won the Emmy Award for comedy series writing in 2018 for the show *The Chi* on the Showtime network. She won an Emmy for outstanding writing (for the episode "Thanksgiving" about a lesbian's coming out experience) on the comedy series *Master of None* on Netflix in 2017. Waithe was executive producer for the horror anthologies series *Them* (2019) on Amazon Prime. She was a screenwriter for the BET series *Boomerang* (2019–2020), and for the Fox network television series *Bones* from 2014 to 2015. Waithe wrote the screenplays for the movies *Beauty* (2022) and *Queen and Slim* (2019). Born and raised in Chicago, she received a BA from Columbia College in Chicago.

Walker, David F. (birthdate unavailable). Comic book writer, filmmaker, and journalist. Walker is an award-wining comic book writer. His work includes a comic series for the old movie character Shaft, a Black detective. His comic *Shaft: A Complicated Man* (Dynamite Entertainment) won the 2015 Glyph Award for the Story of the Year. Walker is the cowriter and cocreator of *NAOMI* (DC Comics) and winner of the Eisner Award for *Bitter Fruit*. Walker has worked for Marvel Comics (*Luke Cage, Occupy Avengers*, and *Power Man and the Iron Fist*, among others). He has worked for DC Comics (*Cyborg*) and Boom! (*Planet of the Apes*).

Wells, Ida B. (July 16, 1862–March 25, 1931). Journalist. Wells was born in Holly Springs, Mississippi, to parents who were enslaved. At the end of slavery and during Reconstruction, Wells received a basic education from the Freedmen's Aid Society and the Episcopal Church. She attended Rust University but dropped out after her parents and younger brother died of yellow fever. She then obtained a teaching certificate and was hired as a teacher. However, upon traveling to Memphis she discovered writing opportunities that she enjoyed more than teaching. She began writing a column under the pen name of Lola. She wrote an article opposing a lynching that led to death threats against her. She fled to New York where she met others with similar political views, and this led to her traveling to England for a short time where she was invited to speak. When she returned to the United States, she continued to write in opposition to lynching and in support of equality and universal suffrage.

West, Cornel (June 2, 1953–). Nonfiction writer and philosopher. West has pursued a path of public intellectual, theologian scholar, and activist. During his academic career, he has taught at Harvard University, Princeton, and Yale. West has twice served as the director of the African American Studies program at Princeton. He holds a bachelor's degree and a doctorate degree from Harvard. West was born in Tulsa, Oklahoma, and was greatly influenced by his grandfather, who was a Baptist minister. West was also influenced by Marxism and the philosophical ideas of Black Theology as reflected in his early publication of *Prophesy Deliverance! An Afro-American Revolutionary Christianity* (1982). His later works include the groundbreaking book on race in the twentieth century, *Race Matters* (1993). In addition, West coauthored, with bell hooks, *Breaking Bread: Insurgent Black Intellectual Life* (1991), and with Henry Louis Gates Jr., *The Future of Race* (1996). He coedited, with Eddie Glaude Jr., *Afro-American Religious Thought* (2003).

Whitehead, Colson (November 6, 1969–). Novelist. Whitehead was born in New York City and lived in various Manhattan neighborhoods. His father and mother both worked in business. Whitehead's aspiration was to become a writer. He graduated from Harvard University with a bachelor's degree in English and comparative literature. After graduating, his first professional position was as a journalist with the *Village Voice*, and then as a writer for *New York Magazine*, *Vibe*, and *Spin*. Whitehead continued to write fiction on his own, and his first novel, *The Intuitionist* (1999), received critical praise although it had gone through years of rejection by prospective publishers. He was able to get it published with a major rewrite, involving the use of an elevator metaphor rather than an escalator metaphor in the book's intersecting themes of race, class, and gender. Whitehead's second novel, *John Henry Days* (2001), won several literary awards including the New York Public Library's Young Lions Fiction Award and the New York Times Book Review Editors' Choice. Whitehead was named the recipient in 2002 of the MacArthur Award of $500,000. He was then able to concentrate his writing efforts to produce three published pieces that received major accolades, a nonfiction book about New York City's spaces titled *The Colossus of New York: A City in Thirteen Parts* (2003), and two novels, *Sag Harbor* (2009) and *Zone One* (2011). In following years, he published five more novels, two of them winning the Pulitzer Prize in consecutive years, *Underground Railroad* and *Nickle Boys*. In addition, *Underground Railroad* won the National Book Award and the Arthur C. Clarke Award for best science fiction novel.

Wilkerson, Isabel (March 8, 1960–). Nonfiction writer and journalist. Wilkerson was the first African American woman to win the Pulitzer Prize and the first African American of any gender to win the Pulitzer Prize for individual reporting. She won the Pulitzer for feature writing in journalism for the story of a small midwestern town cemetery washed away by a flood. Wilkerson wrote her first book, *The Warmth of Other Suns* (2010), about the great migration of Southern Blacks to the urban North between 1915 and 1980—what she has called "the greatest underreported story of the twentieth century." *The Warmth of Other Suns* won the National Book Critics Circle

Award for nonfiction in 2011. Wilkerson's second book, *Caste: The Origins of Our Discontents* (2020), won the inaugural New York University, NYU/Axinn Foundation Prize for a distinguished work in the genre of literary narrative nonfiction. Wilkerson was born in Washington, D.C. Her parents both had migrated from the South, her father from Virginia and her mother from Georgia. She received a bachelor's degree in journalism from Howard University. Wilkerson worked for the *New York Times* as the Chicago bureau chief, and during her free time she conducted years of ethnographic research and interviewed hundreds of migrants. Wilkerson received a Guggenheim Award that allowed her to do extensive background research about the great migration. In her book, she focused on the individual motivations and determination of persons who left the South in search of a better life.

Williams, Saul (February 29, 1972–). Poet, rapper, and spoken word artist. Williams was born in Newburg, New York, the youngest of three children. His father was a Baptist minister, and his mother was a grade-school teacher. Williams holds a BA from Morehouse, where he studied acting and philosophy, and a MFA from New York University. He entered onto the stage of spoken word through the scene of New York cafes, where in 1996 he won the grand championship slam (a term for competitions between poets doing live performance of their own spoken word poetry) at the Nuyorican Poets Café followed by a four-day National Poetry Slam held in Portland, Oregon. Williams then appeared in the documentary *SlamNation*, followed by an award-winning performance in the feature film *Slam*, which he cowrote. Over the decades of his long career, he continued to accept acting roles for the small and big screen. Williams contributed to the albums of an eclectic list of musical artists including NAS, Nine Inch Nails, DJ Krust, KRS-One, Blackalicious, and Janelle Monae. In addition, he has released six albums of his own and published six books of poetry.

Wilson, August (April 27, 1945–October 2, 2005). Playwright. Wilson was born with the name Frederick August Kittle in Pittsburg, Pennsylvania. He changed his name when he was twenty years old. His parents were working-class poor who suffered both racism and classism. His father was a White baker who had emigrated from Germany at childhood. His mother was an African American cleaning woman from North Carolina. Wilson seldom saw his father, who was mainly absent from the family. His mother eventually obtained a divorce and remarried. Although Wilson was a good student, he dropped out of high school during his junior year after transferring to different schools and experiencing repeated incidents of racism. Wilson was an avid reader, and his education was largely self-taught. In addition, he learned the culture and vernacular language of the African American community that he would later depict in his playwriting by observing everyday life, talking with older men, and listening to blues music, which he collected. Wilson's major achievement was a series of ten plays that chronicle the African American experience over each decade of the twentieth century. He wrote the plays between 1980 and 2005. During Wilson's lifetime, eight of his plays reached Broadway, six of them under the direction of Lloyd Richards, who had become Broadway's first African American director with the production of *Raisin in the Sun*. Four of Wilson's plays won the New York Drama Critics Circle Award. He received his first Tony Award for *Ma Rainey's Black Bottom* (1984–1985). Wilson won the Pulitzer Prize for drama and a Tony Award for best play for *Fences* (1987–1988). His later play *The Piano Lesson* (1990–1991) won Wilson his second Pulitzer and his second Tony Award. His plays *Joe Turner's Come and Gone* (1988) and *Two Trains Running* (1992) were both nominees for Tony Awards for best play, as was *Seven Guitars* (1996).

Woodson, Jacqueline (February 12, 1963–). Children's and young adult fiction writer. Woodson won a lifetime achievement honor, the American Library Association's 2006 Margaret A. Edwards Lifetime Award, at age 43, at which time she had published more than twenty books, and then, about ten years later she had published a total of nearly thirty books. Woodson has published two adult novels, that include *Red at the* Bone (2019), and one memoir. Woodson's memoir was written in verse *Black Girl Dreaming* (2014) and won the Newbery Honor Medal. Woodson was named, in 2015 and 2016), the Young People's Poet Laureate. In 2018–2019, Woodson was named the National Ambassador for Young People's Literature. Woodson has won numerous top awards including the 2020 MacArthur Award, The Hans Christian Anderson Award, The Astrid Lindgren Memorial Award, and the Coretta Scott King Award. Woodson was born in Columbus, Ohio and lived some of her youngest years in Greenville, South, Carolina. At age seven the family moved to Brooklyn, New York where Woodson grew up.

Index

Note: Page numbers followed by *f* indicate figures.

ACRL/AASL Interdivisional Committee on Information Literacy Toolkit, Collaboration Checklist, 38–39*f*

ACT-SO (Afro-Academic, Cultural, Technological and Scientific Olympics), 44–45

Adventures of Beekle, The (Santat), 105

African American authors: in American literature, 3–4; list of names, 4–5; promotion of, xiii*f*, 4–6, 17–18, 105–107; steps to follow in promoting, 4–12

African American Read-In (AARI); author's first exposure to, x–xi; descriptions of local observance of, 19–27; national celebration's origin, mission, and growth, xi, 17–19; program format suggestions for, 26–27; Springfield African American Read-In, 17, 22–23, 25, 29–30, 35–41

African American writers. *See* African American authors

Alexander, Kwame, 105

All Boys Aren't Blue (Johnson), 73

Allen, Devin, 74

Alvarez, Julia, 74

American Library Association (ALA) Core Values of Librarianship, 82–83

Angelou, Maya, 56, 60–61

Annie Allen (Brooks), 61

Archive Library Information Center (ALIC), 106

Assessment, 81–94: definitions of, 81–83; examples of, 83–91; general rules, 91–92; purposes, 92–94; qualitative tools, 83, 92; quantitative tools, 83

Association for the Study of African American Life and History (ASALH), 7

Audience, 2, 19, 21, 81, 83–85, 90–93, 96

Author Awards and African American writers, 64–65

Aydin, Andrew, 7, 74

Baker, Calvin, 76

Banaji, Mahzarin R., 72

Baraka, Amiri, 61

Bartley Decatur Neighborhood Center, 33

Beauty in Breaking, The (Harper), 76
Begin Again (Glaude), 76
Belafonte, Harry, 56
Bethune, Mary McLeod, 7
Bishop, Rudine Sims, 50
Black Caucus of the American Library
    Association (BCALA) Literary
    Awards, 64; organizational
    partnership, 75–76
Black Curtain, 44
Black History Month, 7
Black Voices Series, 75–76
Bloomington, Indiana, 62–63
Book reviews in journals, 64
Brinson, Sabrina, 23, 3
Broadside Press Collection, 56–60
Brooks, Gwendolyn, 60–61
Brown, Nicholas, 70–77
Burnout, 9, 99

Caines-Coggswell, Gladys, 23
Caldecott Award, 105
Calypso Music in Postwar America
    Traveling Exhibit, 56
Center for Children's and Young Adult
    Literature (CCYAL), 31
Chancellor, Renate, 74
Children's Literature Festival of the
    Ozarks, 40–41
Colbert, Brandy, 26
Collier, Bryan, 43
Columbus State University (Columbus,
    Georgia), 23–25
Communities, 9–12, 61
Community engagement: definition of,
    13; partnerships and, 41, 49–50;
    used to identify local writers, 65
Competencies of Programming
    Librarians, 98–99
Cooper, J. California, 61
Cooper, Regina Greer, 36
Cooperative Children's Book Center
    (CCBC), 101–102
Coretta Scott King Book Awards, 64

Cosby, Charlotte, 26
COVID-19 pandemic, ix, 53, 67, 70,
    74–75, 77–78
Crispus Attucks High School archival
    collection, 106
Crossover, The (Alexander), 105
Cruz, Angie, 74
Cultural competence. *See* Cultural
    literacy
Cultural literacy, 3, 34, 50, 81–82, 116
Culturally Responsive Evaluation, 91
Culture keepers, 4–5

Davis, Ossie, x
Davis, Phyllis, 36
Dee, Ruby, x, 61
Dewey, John, 96
DiAngelo, Robin, 72
Diversity, 1–2, 11, 34, 116
Dove, Rita, 60–61
Drury University, 6, 22
Duane G. Meyer Library, 36
Du Bois, W. E. B., 54–55

E. J. Josey (Chancellor), 74
Emporia State University (ESU), ix
England, Nora, 49
Ethnography, ix, 117
Exhibits, 60

Faison, Vernice Riddick, 45–47, 53,
    67–70
Feedback, summing-up sessions, 90
Ford, AG, 35–37
Ford, Stephen, 42–43
Funk, Ray, 56

Glaude, Eddie S., Jr., 76
Grande, Reyna, 74

Hardin, Charlotte, 49
Harper, Michele, 76
Herrera, Juan Felipe, 74
Heyward, Shanika, 53, 65–67

Holler If You Hear Me, 62
Holt, Nicole, 6
How the World Was Passed (Smith), 75
How to Be an Antiracist (Kendi), 73
Hughes, Langston, 43, 61
Hurston, Zora Neale, 61

Ikpi, Bassey, 76
I'm Telling the Truth but I'm Lying (Ikpi), 76
Indiana University (IU), x–xi, 20–21; African American and African Diaspora Studies Department, 56, 100; African American Arts Institute, x, 100; African American Popular Music and Culture Archives/Center, 56; Archives of Traditional Music, 56; Black Culture Center, x; Black Culture Center Library, 62; Black Film Center/Archive, 56; Folklore and Ethnomusicology Department, 56; Groups Program, 100–101; John W. Ashton Center, x; Latin American and Caribbean Studies Department, 56; Main Library, x; Multicultural Initiative Grant, 56; Office of Multicultural Affairs, 63; Student Activities Office, 63; Theatre Department, 62, 100
Indianapolis Public Library, 65–67
Intentionality: definitions of, 95, 97; in library programs and services, 100–101, 105–107
Inter-cultural Communication, 11, 34, 50

Jackson, Melvin, Jr., 74
Johnson, George M., 73
Johnson, Javon, 44
Jones, Michelle E., 23–25

Kendi, Ibram X., 72–75

Lamar, Kendrick, 43, 61
Larsen, Nella, 61
Lawrence, Kansas, ix
Lederer Collection, 106
Lewis, John, 7–8, 74
Library Outreach, x, 1, 3–4, 14, 60, 63, 81, 90
Life on Mars (Smith), 61
Lifelong Learning, 11, 34, 50, 77, 116
Lilly Library, xii, 54–57
Limited Editions Club Collection, 55–57
Lincoln University (Pennsylvania), 58–60
Literacy, 2, 81
Local African American writers, 66–67
Lofton, Ferba, 6
Long, Erika, 31–32
Look Both Ways (Reynolds), 75
Lyles, Alana, 6

March (Lewis and Aydin), 7–8
Marshall, Francis, x
Marshall, Gwendolyn, 49
McKesson, DeRay, 74
McKissack, Patricia, 35, 40
Meyers, Walter Dean, 61
Miami University of Ohio: author's place of employment, x; Miami University Museum of Art, 36
Missouri State University, xi, 6, 22, 33, 100–101
Monroe County Public Library (Bloomington), x
Moore, Marty, 35–36
Moore, Wes, 6
More Perfect Reunion (Baker), 76
Morris, Gloria, 6
Morrison, Toni (Chloe Anthony Wofford), 61–62, 83
Multicultural collections, 2, 101–102, 104, 116
Myers, Vernā, 72

NAACP, Springfield, MO Branch, 22, 33

NAACP Image Awards, 64

National African American Museum of History and Culture, 63

National Council of Teachers of English (NCTE), xi, 3–5, 40; Black Caucus of, 3

National Endowment for the Arts, 44

National Impact of Library Public Programs Assessment (NILPPA), 1, 98–99

National School Library Standards, 102

Neal, Marcellus, x

Neal Marshall Black Culture Center (NMBCC): descriptions of, x, 62–63, 100–101; NMBCC Library, 2, 56; NMBCC Library Evening Extravaganza, 47–48, 62–63; NMBCC Library student protest opposing closing, 107–110

Newberry Award, 105

North Carolina Central University (Durham), 45–47, 67–70

Other Wes Moore, The (Moore), 6–7

Ozarks Literacy Council, 41

PanoramaProject.org study on public library programs, 103–104

Partnerships: benefits of, 49–50, 115; common goals, 40–41; definition of, 12; descriptions of xiii*f*, 29–51; K–16 (kindergarten through senior year of college), 30–40; in local communities, 9–12, 50–51; potential partners list, 50–51; school librarians and academic librarians, 38–40

Penumbra Theatre Company, 106

Peoples, Christine, 36

Phillips, Roberta, 70–77

Pieces I Am, The, 62

Pitts, Leonard, Jr., 75

Poetry Foundation, 44

Poetry Out Loud, 44

Poetry readings, 41–45

Poetry slam, 44

Population, U.S., 1

Power-Carter, Stephanie, xi, 20–21

Prince George's County Memorial Library System (PGCMLS), 70–77

Programming: assessment of, 6; cultural, 77; diversity on university campuses, 63; increases in number of, 100; partnerships for, 4–7, 77; programming librarian; 1; promotion of, 6–7; steps for development of, 4

Programs, 1, 26–27, 61

Protocols, 12–13, 34–35

Public libraries, 11

Public library programming events, 103–104

Public service scholarship, 101

Publishers, African American and other minority-owned, 104

Publishing of African American writers, 103

#PublishingPaidMe, 103

Quinn, Nate, 6

Randall, Dudley, 58

Reading, 2–3, 116

Reale, Michelle, 99

Reflective practice. See Reflectivity

Reflectivity: definitions of, 96–97; examples of librarians reflective practice, 97–99; reflective journaling, 99

Reynolds, Jason, 75

Robbins, Steve L., 72

Salisbury University (Salisbury, Maryland), 42–43

Santat, Dan, 105

School libraries, 9–12, 102

Scott, Jerrie Cobb, xi, 18

Scott-Branch, Jamillah, 45–47, 53, 67–70

Seventh Octave, The (Williams), 62

Shaiman, Jason E., 36

Shakur, Tupac, 61, 62

She (Williams), 62

Slam, 62

Smith, Clint, 75

Smith, Tracy K., 60–61

Social capital, 12–14

Sotilleo, Sophia, 56–60

Souls of Black Folk, The (Du Bois), 55

Springfield Multicultural Festival, 41

Springfield Public Schools, 22, 25, 35, 41

Springfield-Greene County Library District, 22, 25, 41

Stamped (Reynolds), 75

Students, 49

Telling a People's Story Exhibit, 35–37

Thomas, R. Eric, 73

Thomas, Rosalyn, 49

Thomas and Beulah (Dove), 61

Thomas-Tate, Shurita, 32–34

Tibbs, Gloria, 21

Trethewey, Natasha, 74

Tubbs, Anna Malaika, 74

UJIMA Language and Literacy, 32–34

Umbra Search African American History, 106

University libraries, 11

University of Kansas (KU), ix

University of Minnesota, 106

University of Missouri in Kansas City (UMKC), ix, 21

Untamed Tongues, 44

Vinson, Taylor, 44

Walker, Alice, 60–61

Walker, Tricia Elam, 74

Watson Library, ix

We Need Diverse Books (WNDB), 3, 103

Websites with frequent coverage of Black writers, 64–65

Whittenberger Auditorium, 63

Wilkerson, Isabel, 74

Williams, Saul, 62–63

Wilson, August, 83

Woodburn Hall, 62

Woodson, Carter G., 7

Youth, 1–3; postmillennials, 1; as program partners, 49–50; and students, 10–11

Zoboi, Ibi, 32

About the Author

GRACE M. JACKSON-BROWN is a professor for research and instruction at Missouri State University Libraries in Springfield, Missouri. She is chairperson of the Springfield African American Read-In and recipient of the 2014 Zora Neale Hurston Award for promoting African American literature and the Educational Partnership Award of the NAACP Springfield Chapter. Her career spans more than twenty-five years as an academic librarian, much of it devoted to library outreach diversity programming at two universities. She holds a master's degree in library and information management from Emporia State University, Emporia, Kansas, and a PhD in mass communication from Indiana University-Bloomington.